pathfinder guide

Hampshire *and the* New Forest

WALKS

Compiled by
Jenny Plucknett

D1462567

JARROLD

Ordnance
Survey

Acknowledgements

I should like, first of all, to thank my fellow walkers Les Broomfield, Chris Matcham, Stan Waterman and Fran and Pedro Prá-Lopez for their enjoyable company. I should also like to thank Colin Piper, Hampshire County Council's Rights-of-Way Manager. Others who shared their walks with me so that I could include them in this book and whom I should like to thank are Joan Grant, Bob Webb and the Romsey and Alton groups of the Ramblers' Association. The publishers also thank John Cawley of the Eastleigh Ramblers for valuable help in updating routes.

Text:	Jenny Plucknett
Photography:	Jarrold Publishing, Jenny Plucknett, p. 66 by Peter Titmuss for the Southern Tourist Board
Editor:	Geoffrey Sutton
Designers:	Brian Skinner, Doug Whitworth

Series Consultant: Brian Conduit

Jarrold Publishing   ISBN 0-7117-0609-3

While every care has been taken to ensure the accuracy of the route directions, the publishers cannot accept responsibility for errors or omissions, or for changes in details given. The countryside is not static: hedges and fences can be removed, field boundaries can be altered, footpaths can be rerouted and changes in ownership can result in the closure or diversion of some concessionary paths. Also, paths that are easy and pleasant for walking in fine conditions may become slippery, muddy and difficult in wet weather, while stepping-stones across rivers and streams may become impassable.

If you find an inaccuracy in either the text or maps, please write to Jarrold Publishing at the address below.

First published 1993
by Jarrold Publishing and Ordnance Survey
Revised and reprinted 1996, 2000

Printed in Belgium
by Proost NV, Turnhout. 3/00

Jarrold Publishing
Pathfinder Guides, Whitefriars, Norwich NR3 1TR
E-mail: pathfinder@jarrold.com

Front cover: Bucklers Hard
Previous page: Beaulieu Palace House

Contents

Short, easy walks

Walks of modest length, likely to involve some modest uphill walking

More challenging walks which may be longer and/or over more rugged terrain, often with some stiff climbs

Keymap

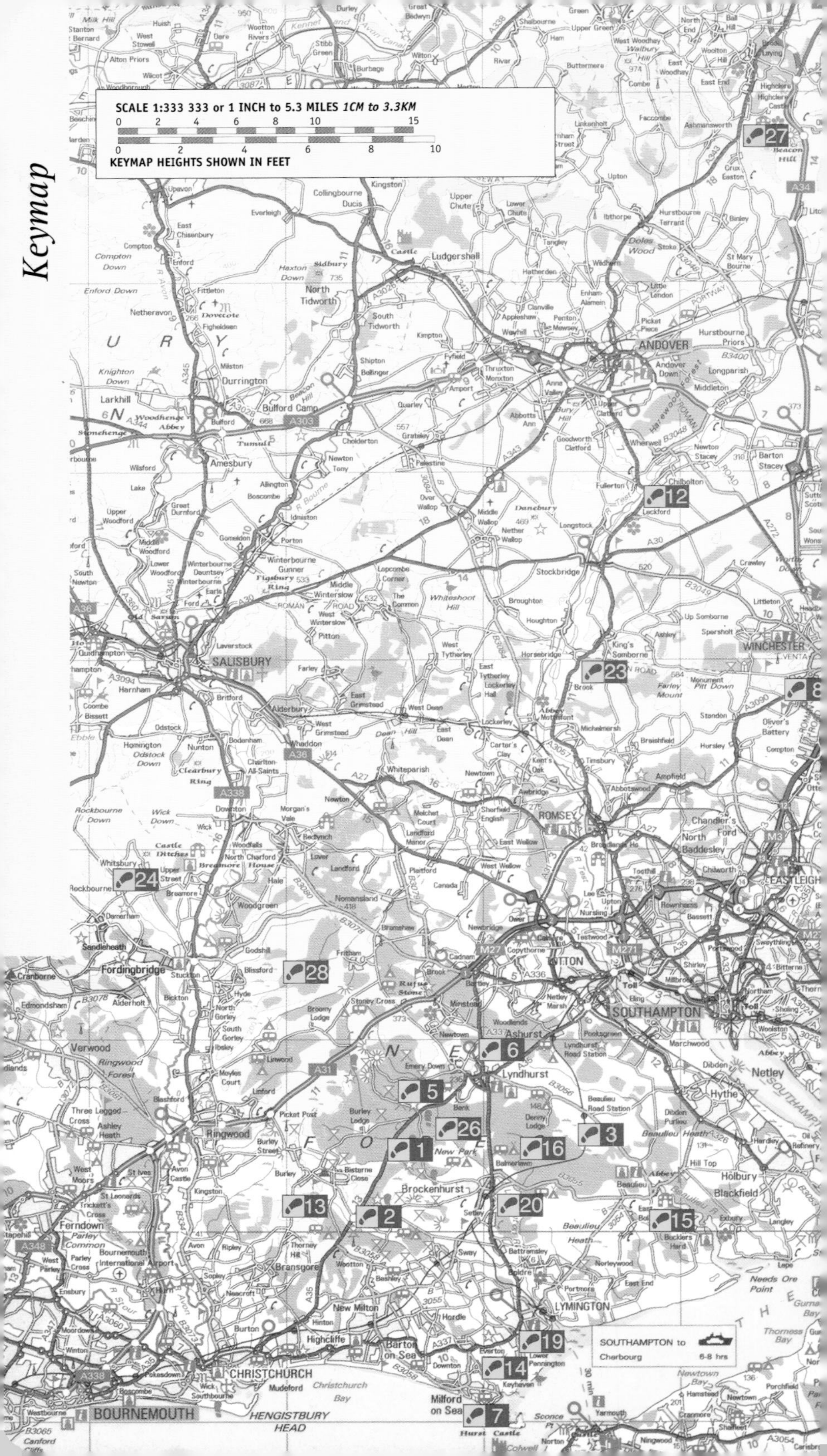

SCALE 1:333 333 or 1 INCH to 5.3 MILES 1CM to 3.3KM
0 2 4 6 8 10 15
0 2 4 6 8 10
KEYMAP HEIGHTS SHOWN IN FEET
SOUTHAMPTON to Cherbourg 6-8 hrs
ANDOVER
SALISBURY
ROMSEY
WINCHESTER
EASTLEIGH
SOUTHAMPTON
TOTTON
LYMINGTON
CHRISTCHURCH
BOURNEMOUTH
Ringwood
Fordingbridge
Lyndhurst
Brockenhurst
Amesbury
Stockbridge
Ludgershall
Durrington
Highcliffe
Milford on Sea
HENGISTBURY HEAD
Christchurch Bay
Hurst Castle
Beaulieu
Hythe
Netley
Ferndown
Verwood
Cranborne

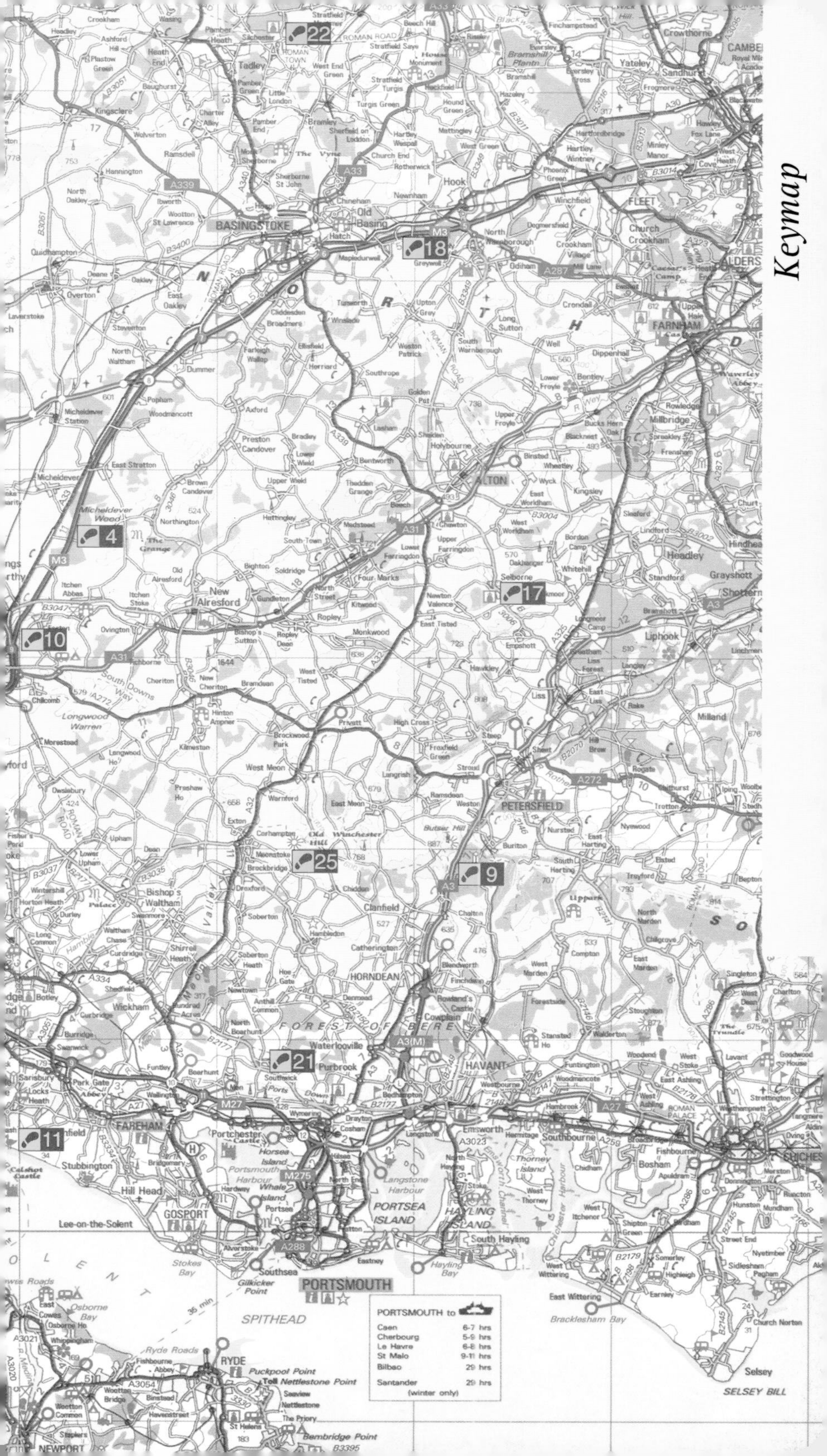

Keymap

PORTSMOUTH to

Caen	6-7 hrs
Cherbourg	5-9 hrs
Le Havre	6-8 hrs
St Malo	9-11 hrs
Bilbao	29 hrs
Santander (winter only)	29 hrs

BASINGSTOKE

FARNHAM

ALTON

PETERSFIELD

HORNDEAN

HAVANT

FAREHAM

GOSPORT

PORTSMOUTH

Southsea

SPITHEAD

RYDE

NEWPORT

SELSEY BILL

FOREST OF BERE

PORTSEA ISLAND

HAYLING ISLAND

SOLENT

Walk	Page	Start	Nat. Grid Reference	Distance	Time
Beaulieu River	46	Beaulieu village	SU 386021	5¾ miles (9.3km)	3–3½ hrs
Bishop's Dyke, New Forest	16	Beaulieu Road Station	SU 362050	3¼ miles (5.2km)	1½ hrs
Brockenhurst old church and Ivy Wood	61	Brockenhurst	SU 315024	6¼ miles (10.1km)	3–3½ hrs
Busketts Lawn Inclosure	22	Woodlands (A35)	SU 310111	3¾ miles (6km)	2 hrs
Greywell and the Basingstoke Canal	55	North Warnborough	SU 728517	6¼ miles (10.1km)	4½ hrs
Highland Water, New Forest	80	Balmer Lawn, Brockenhurst	SU 302030	8 miles (12.9km)	4½–5 hrs
Holmsley old railway and Whitten Pond	42	Holmsley	SU 221010	5¼ miles (8.4km)	3 hrs
Knightwood Oak and New Forest reptiliary	20	Millyford Bridge	SU 267078	3¼ miles (5.2km)	2 hrs
Lymington saltmarshes and estuary	58	Lymington	SZ 326956	6¼ miles (10.1km)	2½–3 hrs
Meeting of the rivers Anton and Test	39	Fullerton	SU 383389	5½ miles (8.9km)	3½ hrs
Micheldever Wood archaeological trail	18	Micheldever Wood	SU 529362	3 miles (4.8km)	2 hrs
Milford on Sea	24	Milford on Sea	SZ 291917	3½ miles (5.6km)	2 hrs
Naked Man and Wilverley Inclosure	14	Wilverley Inclosure	SU 253010	2¾ miles (4.4km)	1½–2 hrs
North New Forest: Fritham to Abbot's Well	86	Fritham	SU 230140	10½ miles (17km)	6 hrs
Old Winchester Hill and Garden Hill Lane	77	Old Winchester Hill	SU 646213	8 miles (12.9km)	4½ hrs
Pennington Marshes	44	Keyhaven harbour	SZ 306915	6 miles (9.7km)	3 hrs
Portsmouth and the Wayfarers' Walk	64	Purbrook Heath	SU 669078	6½ miles (10.5km)	4–4½ hrs
Queen Elizabeth Country Park	30	Petersfield	SU 718181	4¼ miles (6.8km)	2½ hrs
Rhinefield ornamental trees	12	Brockenhurst	SU 267047	2¼ miles (3.6km)	1½–2 hrs
River Itchen	33	Kings Worthy	SU 493323	4¾ miles (7.6km)	3 hrs
River Test near King's Somborne	71	Horsebridge	SU 344304	7 miles (11.3km)	5 hrs
Rockbourne and Whitsbury	74	Rockbourne	SU 114181	6¾ miles (10.9km)	4½ hrs
St Cross Hospital to Winchester Cathedral	27	St Cross village	SU 475278	4 miles (6.4km)	2½–3 hrs
Selborne and Noar Hill	52	Selborne village	SU 742335	5¼ miles (8.4km)	3–3½ hrs
Silchester and the Roman town	67	Silchester	SU 643623	6¾ miles (10.9km)	4½ hrs
Southampton Water	36	Fleetend	SU 505058	5 miles (8km)	3 hrs
Standing Hat, New Forest	49	Brockenhurst	SU 314035	6 miles (9.7km)	3 hrs
Wayfarers' Walk, Ashmansworth	83	Ashmansworth	SU 410566	9½ miles (15.3km)	6–6½ hrs

Comments

This easy walk follows the route of a picturesque river towards the estuary and the Solent. It starts from an unspoilt country village and visits a now tiny but once important shipbuilding centre.

A wetland with a fascinating past is easily crossed on duckboards as part of a half-day walk that also encompasses typical New Forest scenery of streams, heathland and ancient woodland.

An ideal walk for a spring morning, this route follows a lane to visit the New Forest's most ancient church. It returns via a nature reserve and woodland where wild flowers add splashes of clear colour.

A short and easy Christmas tree walk for winter on the eastern side of the New Forest but take waterproof footwear if it is, or has been, wet.

This is a beautiful country walk for a sunny, summer day. It abounds with natural history interest and includes a return via a section of this popular canal's towpath.

A tranquil walk that follows a forest river through ancient, unspoilt woodland, now a wildlife reserve. The return route is via gravel tracks and wide lawns kept well mown by the New Forest's wild ponies.

Some flowers bloom most of the year to add colour to this easily followed route over heather-clothed heathland that returns along the route of a disused New Forest railway line.

A short woodland walk that provides the chance to visit three fascinating local places of interest.

An easy and mainly flat walk through the quieter side streets of this pretty old town to finally reach the water and follow the estuary edge back via the modern yacht haven and old town quay.

This walk gently rises and falls, meandering through fields and two river valleys with their old water meadows and fast-running water.

Bluebells colour the woodland floor in late spring on this short walk. A wood, together with still visible even more ancient settlements, has probably existed here as far back as the 5th or 6th century.

An easy route that follows the sea edge and a cliff path providing views of one of the entrances to the Solent and returning via the ancient village church, then through the village centre set around a green.

Mainly easy walking on gravel tracks and wide grass rides, this short New Forest route passes the remains of a tree that once had a macabre use.

This is a long but ideal route for an easy stroll after wet weather as it mainly follows gravel tracks with good views at its western end.

A route to please those with a bias to ancient and natural history alike. The hill provides wide views, with a route that follows an ancient path and then meanders through two pretty villages.

For those interested in unusual migratory birds this is a walk for spring or autumn. It starts via a country lane to reach and return via a new sea wall that divides the estuary from the marshes behind.

Rolling farmland provides the main background for this walk which highlights the forts designed a century ago to protect Portsmouth from invasion.

Ideal for a summer day out at this East Hampshire country park these two short but very different walks can be done on the same day or independently.

A short and easy wintertime New Forest walk with its well-established route and giant conifers. This area is also worth a visit in late spring when the wild rhododendron bushes nearby are in flower.

An easy walk along field and and village paths through three small riverside hamlets. It ends alongside, then crossing, this attractive and renowned trout river.

A beautiful walk at any time of the year with a route that criss-crosses this stunning trout river and ambles along a disused railway line and through farmland with a fascinating history.

A walk through central Hampshire's typically gentle rounded countryside, this route leaves the pretty village and ancient church to follow old farm tracks and cross rolling downland with some good views.

A delightful short riverside route that takes the walker straight into Winchester's historic centre, returning via a hedge-lined path and quiet roads.

The renowned 18th-century vicar of this attractive village ensured its popularity. The walk's uphill route provides fine views and the track descends via a path constructed by the vicar and his brother.

An easy walk that allows those with imagination a view of the once prosperous Roman town now hidden below fields but still surrounded by impressive walls.

Waterproof footwear is advised after rain for this gentle and unspoilt route along gravel tracks and through a nature reserve which then follows the beach edge with views across the busy waterway.

A flat and easy, but sometimes muddy, woodland route. Apart from the periodic noise of trains a lack of dwellings and made-up roads ensure that this is a good place to hear and see local wildlife.

A stunning and more strenuous walk that is ideal for a calm and clear day. The route goes over some of Hampshire's highest northern countryside, offering some superb views.

At-a-glance...

Introduction to Hampshire and the New Forest

The rich variety in Hampshire's landscape makes walking in the county specially rewarding. It is a countryside of gentle contrasts which, for the most part, is surprisingly unspoilt.

The Natural Framework

North Hampshire, just south of heavily populated areas like Newbury and Reading, has a clay or sandy soil but this soon gives way to the rolling downland of mid Hampshire. This chalkland, covering just under half the county, is used mainly for farming. Apart from cereals, other commonly grown crops are rape and more latterly flax (linseed), grown for their oil and as animal feed. These share the land with herds of cattle, some sheep, free-range pigs, horses and a few goats. South through this area run some of Britain's most famous trout rivers: the Test, the Itchen and the Meon. Here the clear, sparkling water allows exciting views of beautifully coloured, patterned and often giant fish. The rivers also provide an ideal habitat for a wealth of wildlife and for one of Hampshire's most ancient products, watercress.

Attractive, centuries-old villages nestle in the softly contoured valleys. Traditional houses are constructed of local brick and flint, and these homes blend into their surroundings, lying side-by-side with pastel-tinted thatched cottages. Now, in many places, these older homes are interspersed with brasher 20th-century houses and bungalows. Sadly, the post office, shop and school – the heart of many of these villages – have closed to become additional housing. But the village church remains to give a central focus, and the pub still provides an important stopping point for the wayfarer.

The only steep hills in Hampshire – and these do not compare in size with those in many other counties – are the Hampshire Hangers. These hills run north from Petersfield to Alton and, in the main, trees cling to the cliff-like sides. The Hangers and, in the north of the county, the North Hampshire Ridgeway provide walks with panoramic views.

The Isle of Wight protects some of the land in the south of the county, allowing soft fruits, vines and greenhouses of tomatoes, nursery stock, house plants and flowers to predominate.

Hampshire's coastline, some sand and some shingle, includes outstanding natural harbours. Here stand the ports of Southampton and Portsmouth. Smaller estuaries, particularly those of partially navigable rivers, have become sites for marinas, and sailing is a popular leisure activity at Lymington, Hamble and on the Beaulieu River. Along the coast, other water sports such as windsurfing and water-skiing are popular.

The New Forest is the jewel in Hampshire's natural crown. Poor soil of soft sand and clay is one of the reasons for its survival relatively unchanged for centuries, and its ancient woods, heathlands and bogs now make it important as one of the few remaining sanctuaries for some of Britain's rarer wildlife.

Historic Heritage

Hampshire's long history provides walkers with many points of interest. Popular with the Romans, Hampshire still has many signs of their residence. Winchester was the fifth-largest walled city in Roman Britain, and roads radiated to other nearby centres. These were Sarum, near the present Salisbury, Portchester at Portsmouth, Southampton, and Calleva Atrebatum, near Silchester in the north, now buried beneath green fields but surrounded by striking ramparts. However, Hampshire's history goes many centuries further back than this. Burial mounds, up to 4500 years old, and earthworks, like that on Old Winchester Hill, provide the walker with evidence of these early inhabitants.

The county's name comes from Southampton's 7th-century Saxon name 'Hamtun' – *ham*, land by a river, and *tun*, a village. Later, Alfred the Great, who became king in 871, made Winchester his capital, and in 1194 Richard the Lionheart was crowned here. Winchester, originally a Celtic settlement, contains little sign of its Roman period as most of the buildings are buried below the present city, although the streets still run along the original Roman routes. However, many other signs of Winchester's historic past can still be seen, including two of the original gateways that led into the medieval city, Winchester College, founded in the 14th century and the oldest English public school and, of course, Winchester Cathedral.

In the 18th and 19th centuries, Hampshire prospered. The county's salt industry, which dates back to the 11th century, reached its high point, and local clay provided the raw material for a thriving brick and building industry. Grand houses were built or extended, many of which are now open to the public. Portsmouth, an important naval centre from earliest times, and the tiny Bucklers Hard in the New Forest used local oaks to build great warships. The Basingstoke Canal was constructed in 1794, and from the mid 19th century a railway allowed people to travel from London to Dorchester through the New Forest, bringing visitors to the county and prosperity to seaside resorts.

Through the ages Hampshire has had close ties with the navy and the army. Apart from centres like Portsmouth, the New Forest played a surprisingly important role in the wars of this century. Brockenhurst became a centre for Indian and Canadian wounded in the 1914–18 war. In the 1939–45 war three main and several smaller air bases were located in the forest, and troops massed here for the D-day landings, well hidden amongst the cover.

The second half of the 20th century brought large industries to Hampshire. At Fawley, are the massive Esso oil refinery, the giant Fawley power station, a plastics factory and Rechem, a chemical waste disposal company. At the same time Basingstoke and Andover expanded as important industrial centres.

The Tall Trees route at Rheinfield Drive

Wildlife Riches

Due mainly to the wide range of habitats in Hampshire it is one of the richest counties in the country for wildlife. For those interested in flora or fauna many of these walks will provide the sharp-eyed with thrilling viewing.

The county contains about one-tenth of the national total of ancient and semi-natural woodland, nearly double the average for most other counties. Because of their age these woods are specially rich in wildlife.

Much of the chalk downland has been improved for agricultural use but where it is too steep and where downland has been preserved as nature reserves the land is rich in wild flowers in summer. The flowers in turn draw a large insect population, including many butterflies. Also in Hampshire you will find grassland, heather-covered heaths and a wide range of wetlands that include not only those famous chalk rivers but canals, reservoirs, lakes, bogs and fens. The coastal marshes and mudflats, such as Farlington in the east and Keyhaven in the west of the county, are internationally important both for breeding birds and winter migrants. Plant species found in Hampshire number over 1400 – the greatest number of any county in England.

The New Forest is home to some national rarities such as a few remaining sand lizards and smooth snakes. Others, like the wild gladiolus and the New Forest cicada, are found nowhere else in the country.

The New Forest

The history and the poor soil of the New Forest have allowed it to remain relatively untouched – certainly unique in Western Europe. William I created his Nova Foresta in 1079. Since then the forest has been protected because the groups of people most closely associated with it have conflicting interests and fairly equally balanced powers. The commoners, with a right to graze their animals on the forest, have played a vital role since early times in ensuring that the balance of grazing land to woodland is maintained. If an area is planted with trees and enclosed, another area must be opened up for the use of stock: forest ponies, cattle, donkeys and, in the last few years, sheep.

Protecting the New Forest is now in the hands of the New Forest Committee, which brings together six main groups. These are the Forestry Commission, acting for the Crown; the Verderers on behalf of the commoners; the Countryside Commission and English Nature to ensure wildlife is a priority; and New Forest District Council and Hampshire County Council, who aim to protect the interests of local people and of tourism.

Care of the New Forest – *Special Points from the Forestry Commission*

Few places in Britain provide such wonderful opportunities for public access as the New Forest. The Crown land extends over more than 100 square miles (260 sq km) and since 1924 has been managed by the Forestry Commission. Today they seek to balance the diverse and sometimes conflicting demands of wildlife conservation with public access for recreation, as well as the needs of the commoners, who graze their animals on the open forest, and timber production. This is a working, living landscape, much in the public eye and, as leisure opportunities continue to multiply for us all, the New Forest is increasingly the focus for more potentially harmful forms of recreational access.

The Forestry Commission provides over 140 public car parks and ten camping sites throughout the New Forest. More than twenty years ago the decision was made to close off most of the open forest to vehicle access, and 'wild' camping was forbidden. The benefits to the environment have been considerable.

Safe, easy access to virtually all of the New Forest is now provided for the car-borne visitor, allowing freedom to wander and enjoy the forest's magnificent ancient woodland, peaceful streamside lawns and wild heather moorland. We want all our visitors to enjoy and discover for themselves the special qualities which set the New Forest apart as a place for peaceful enjoyment of nature.

The New Forest is ideal walking country but in recent years off-road cycling and horse-riding have rapidly grown in popularity. Freedom to explore inevitably brings with it risks of disturbance to wildlife. Many people enjoy exercising their dogs in the forest. All dog-walkers should be particularly mindful of the potential damage and distress their 'friendly' companions could inflict on forest animals. Hares and all species of deer carry strong scent; heavily pregnant does and young fawns especially are a natural quarry for any dog. Ground-nesting birds – some, like woodlark, begin nest-building in March – are at risk from people and dogs unaware that eggs or young chicks are hidden in the heather.

Every year there are reports of ponies and cattle being attacked and injured by loose dogs. Please ensure that your dog is under control at all times and that those who cycle keep to the gravelled roads.

Enjoy the challenges and opportunities for exploring this unique area. All we ask is

The Balmer Lawn Hotel at Brockenhurst – the D-Day landings HQ

respect for the special character and traditions that have preserved the New Forest and its wildlife through the centuries.

Further Reading

Barton, J. *Hidden Hampshire* (Newbury, Countryside Books, 1989)

Barton, J. *The Visitor's Guide to Hampshire and the Isle of Wight* (Lashbourne, Moorland, 1985)

Draper, J. *Hampshire Curiosities* (Wimbourne, Dovecote Press, 1989)

Heathcote, T. *A Wild Heritage, the History and Nature of the New Forest* (Southampton, Ensign Publications, 1990)

New Forest Book, an Illustrated Anthology, The, ed. J. O'Donald Mays (Ringwood, New Forest Leaves, 1989)

New Hampshire Village Book, The, (Newbury, Countryside Books, & Winchester, Hampshire Federation of Women's Institutes, 1990)

Sibley, P., & Fletcher, R. *Discovering the New Forest* (London, Robert Hale, 1986)

Rhinefield ornamental trees

Start	Rhinefield Drive, Brockenhurst
Distance	2¼ miles (3.6km)
Approximate time	1½ –2 hours
Parking	Forestry Commission Blackwater car park
Refreshments	Pubs, cafés and restaurants in Brockenhurst
Ordnance Survey maps	Landranger 195 (Bournemouth & Purbeck) and Outdoor Leisure 22 (New Forest)

This short walk takes a close look at some of this country's most exotic towering conifers, most planted here in the New Forest in 1859. The route begins along a well-surfaced, waymarked path that is suitable for wheel or push-chairs. It has been laid out by the Forestry Commission to allow people to enjoy these impressive trees at first hand without having to walk along the road.

Leaving the Tall Trees route, well marked with information posts along the way, the walk crosses Rhinefield Drive, a spectacle of flowering rhododendrons in May, to continue on the other side uphill past oak and beech trees. The walk returns along gravel tracks where native trees have been felled to be replaced by younger and smaller conifers, Douglas fir and Norway spruce, planted for commercial use. Finally entering an arboretum, planted one hundred years after the giants of the earlier part of the walk, a wide range of well-spaced young trees from all over the world can be seen. Most are labelled, and it is well worth allowing some time to wander through this deer-fenced enclosure before returning to the car park.

The New Forest is of course not new at all. In fact it has had this name for over 900 years, named *Nova Foresta* by William I in 1079 when he had it set aside as a royal forest to protect the deer for hunting by the royal retinue. The trees on this walk are not specially old in New Forest terms – there are oaks over 300 years old in the forest – but these introduced conifers are among the forest's tallest trees.

Rhinefield Drive, known as the Ornamental Drive, was up until 1938 a gravel track which linked Rhinefield House, a large Tudor-style Victorian house built around 1890, with what is now the A35 Bournemouth to Lyndhurst road. Prior to this, a master keeper's lodge stood on the spot, and the land around was used as a tree nursery. The magnificent trees that now line the drive were planted as an experiment to see which trees would grow well in the local soil and climate. Among those that have flourished are the redwoods and wellingtonias. The tallest wellingtonia is over 165ft (50m) high with a girth of nearly 26ft (8m).

Leave the car park by the narrow gravel path on the left of the WC,

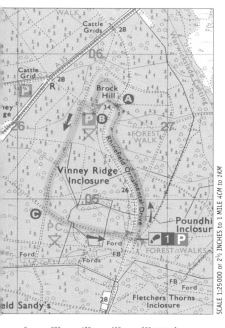

| 0 | 200 | 400 | 600 | 800 METRES | 1 |
| 0 | 200 | 400 | 600 YARDS | | ½ |

KILOMETRES
MILES

following red-banded posts. You will be struck by the height and size of the redwoods mentioned earlier and easily recognised by their orange-red cork-like bark. The tallest redwood known, and thought to be the tallest tree in the world, is in California and is 367ft (111m) tall. Related to the redwood is Rhinefield Drive's most impressive tree, the wellingtonia. This is another native of California, also known as the 'California big tree'. It grows on the western slopes of the Sierra Nevada. Some of these Californian wellingtonias are 4000 years old and around 365ft (110m) high. In fact the trunk of one acts as a tunnel for road traffic! The New Forest trees are amongst the tallest in Great Britain but do not compare with these North American giants.

The path leads past a reconstructed bank and ditch which shows how forest inclosure boundaries were constructed to keep deer for hunting inside and the forest commoners' cattle and ponies out.

Continue along the route, following the red markers. The path passes a bomb crater. There are many of these in the New Forest. In 1944 the forest became a perfect place to conceal vast numbers of troops and vehicles gathering for the D-day invasion of Europe.

Take a timber railed walkway and cross Rhinefield Drive into Brock Hill car park A. This car park gets its name from an ancient badger sett nearby. Badgers – *brock* is the Old English name for them – are protected here, as in many other parts of the country, by a badger group whose members regularly check on the setts.

Go towards the car park entrance and, following a green marker now, take the path up the hill to the right and then left into the trees. When the waymarked path meets a grass ride and turns left, leave the route to turn downhill and right instead B.

This grass ride soon reaches a gravel track, turn left onto it. Continue along the gravel track, past grass rides off to the right and left until a crossroads with another gravel track is reached.

Turn left here C and up to the Blackwater Arboretum entrance. The earliest of these trees, tiny beside their giant neighbours, have now been growing for just over thirty years, but new ones are constantly being added. The deer find young trees irresistible and can quickly destroy them so they are kept out by a 12ft- (3.6m) high fence. Many of the trees are labelled but it is well worth carrying a tree identification book with you if you want to check others.

Cross the arboretum to leave it from a gate on the opposite side and continue straight ahead across Rhinefield Drive and back into the car park. ●

Naked Man and Wilverley Inclosure

Start	Wilverley Inclosure, New Forest
Distance	2¾ miles (4.4km)
Approximate time	1½ –2 hours
Parking	Forestry Commission Wilverley car park
Refreshments	None
Ordnance Survey maps	Landranger 195 (Bournemouth & Purbeck) and Outdoor Leisure 22 (New Forest)

This short walk takes in both woodland and open forest. Most of the earlier section along a woodland route uses undulating gravel tracks but a short section along grass rides can be muddy in wet weather. The walk returns through grassland to pass The Naked Man, a tree, not much more than a stump now, that is surrounded by a fascinating local legend. Fallow deer may be glimpsed crossing the track, and ponies, excluded from the inclosure by fence and gates, enjoy the area of lawn beside the wood, which is also shared with ball-game players and kite-flyers.

A popular spot with local people, this walk starts through an inclosure which has latterly had large areas of conifers removed. Now the sun can reach and warm this open land, and it is fast turning into an expanse of purple when the foxgloves are in bloom.

Go towards the end of the car park and take the gate into the inclosure. Continue straight ahead up the gravel track, passing paths to right and left, until it reaches a T-junction with another gravel track. Turn right here beside a plaque which informs you when this inclosure has been thrown open and when re-enclosed **Ⓐ**.

When William I created the New Forest the local peasants were forbidden to restrain their animals by fencing them in as this would have impeded the free running of hunted deer. This meant that stock could roam freely and they, together with browsing deer, considerably reduced the number of trees. In the Middle Ages it was decided that large areas should be enclosed so that woodland could be re-established. However, when the trees had grown enough to be out of danger from browsing animals, the areas would again be thrown open. Changing acts through the years have decided on how much land can be enclosed and how much must remain open. Today a strict check is still kept, and when one area is enclosed another must be thrown open in recompense.

This gravel track goes downhill to meet a crossroads with a grass ride. Continue on the gravel track which now gently ascends. Ignore a gravel track

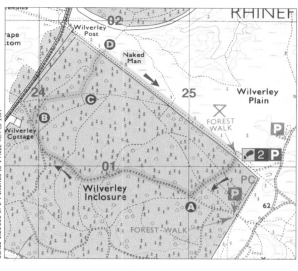

that joins from the left and pass a grass ride off to the right. Through double gates, the main road can be seen ahead. When a second grass ride goes off to the right, shortly before reaching the gates, take this **B**.

The way soon reaches a meeting of grass rides. Take the wide grass ride which you find immediately on your right. This path is soon crossed by a narrower grass path. Turn left onto this **C**. It can be quite muddy here in wet weather.

This path leads to a gate out of the inclosure. On leaving the inclosure, turn right onto a wide grass path **D**.

On the left is a tree stump, surrounded by rails. This is the Naked Man, and it is said that this oak tree was used as a gibbet to hang at least one highwayman. It certainly has been known by this name since the 18th century and, until it crumbled to today's short trunk,

it also extended two naked branches to the sky. Another legend tells of a storm that broke on the night they hanged a man from the tree and that when lightning struck, it tore all his clothes off.

Continue to follow this grass ride alongside the inclosure until it reaches the car park. ●

The fences that surround the New Forest inclosures like Wilverley keep ponies and cattle out but do not restrict the deer

Bishop's Dyke, New Forest

Start	Pig Bush, south-east of Beaulieu Road Station
Distance	3¼ miles (5.2km)
Approximate time	1½ hours
Parking	Forestry Commission Pig Bush car park
Refreshments	Pubs at Beaulieu Road
Ordnance Survey maps	Landranger 196 (Solent & the Isle of Wight) and Outdoor Leisure 22 (New Forest)

This walk allows you to enjoy a typical mixture of New Forest scenery within a surprisingly short distance. It goes across heath and through woodland, then crosses and recrosses Bishop's Dyke, a 13th-century bank and ditch which encircles an area of bog. Duckboards give easy access to the bog and allow a close view of some of the fascinating plants that inhabit this wetland. The gentle sloping heathland that follows is popular with the tiny Dartford warbler with its grey head, red-ringed eye and rust breast. This bird came close to extinction a few years ago in a series of harsh winters. Happily, numbers are now increasing again.

The ponies of the forest are owned by commoners with the right to 'Common of Pasture'. This right, which it is thought goes back to the time when William the Conqueror turned the forest into a hunting preserve, allows a commoner to graze his or her stock on the forest. This is usually ponies but can also be cattle, some donkeys and latterly a few sheep. Ponies are branded with the owner's individual brand so that they can be quickly recognised.

Leave through the wood on the opposite side of the car park to the road, taking a narrow path about halfway along this side. The path soon comes out of the wood on the opposite side. Turn left here and walk along the track that follows the wood edge. This wood contains some examples of the rare 'wild service' tree (*Pyrus torminalis*).

Similar to a maple, the leaves turn deep red in autumn, and the fruits, which are edible only when over ripe, used to be sold in southern England as 'chequers'.

On reaching a T-junction with a shingle path, turn right onto it **A** and cross the bridge over the stream.

Over fourteen different species of tree and shrub can be found to the left beside this stream. Also on the left is Halfpenny Green. There are a number of halfpenny greens in Hampshire, and the name is an apt description of their size. After crossing heathland the path enters a wood. This is always a good area for seeing woodland birds such as woodpecker, tree creeper, wren, tits and nuthatch. Ignore a path from the left and continue ahead **B**.

The path then curves round to the right and comes out of the wood again to become a wide grass ride between bracken. From this ride the bank and ditch mentioned earlier can be seen. Bishop's Dyke encompasses an area of about 500 acres (200 hectares), and it is thought that it was built around 1284. The then Bishop of Winchester, John de Pontoise, was offered an area of land that he could crawl around in a day. It is said that, wanting the largest area possible, he spent twenty-four hours on hands and knees!

The grass ride bears to the left to arrive at a bridge over the main Bournemouth to Southampton railway line. The small fenced enclosure here is a pony pound. Each autumn in the New Forest there are pony round-ups, known as 'The Drifts'. The ponies are herded into these pounds, found throughout the forest, where they are checked, branded and wormed. At this point a pony may be returned to the forest or sent on to the Pony Sales. These sales take place across the way from Beaulieu Road Station in an area of wooden railed pens that can be seen from the road. Some ponies will be bought and broken in for riding but most go to the 'meat men'.

Ignore the track over the railway bridge and instead turn right **C** just before the pony pound onto a narrower grass path. This path takes you back away from the railway, crosses another part of Bishop's Dyke, through conifers, and continues straight ahead to a small footbridge crossing a stream. Ignore a similar bridge to the left. The path runs straight ahead as a sandy track through the heather then crosses bog on duckboards. Due to the acid soil of the New Forest the water from the bog appears dark brown and oily. This is an ideal place to see many bog plants such as the yellow star-flower bog asphodel, lemon-scented bog myrtle and creeping-stemmed bog St John's wort with its bright yellow flowers. The white powder-puff seed-heads of cotton grass appear in summer, and there are tiny insect-eating sundew.

Continue uphill, away from the bog, on a gravel track that once more crosses Bishop's Dyke **D**. Where the path forks, take the left-hand fork and ignore any small paths going off it. Continue ahead towards a small group of trees. Just before reaching the trees, take a path off to the right **E**. This grass path takes you back to the wood behind Pig Bush car park. Before reaching the trees, take a narrow path to the left, which skirts the side of the wood **F**.

Continue uphill on this path beside the wood until the path reaches a lone pine tree. Turn right at the tree onto a narrow track that leads back into the car park. ●

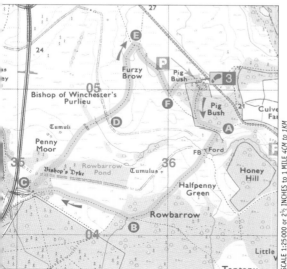

SCALE 1:25000 or 2½ INCHES to 1 MILE 4CM to 1KM

Micheldever Wood archaeological trail

Start	Micheldever Wood, east of the M3
Distance	3 miles (4.8km)
Approximate time	2 hours
Parking	Micheldever Wood Forestry Enterprise car park, between A33 and Northington
Refreshments	None
Ordnance Survey maps	Landranger 185 (Winchester & Basingstoke), Explorer 132 (Winchester, New Alresford & East Meon)

This short but fascinating walk takes a route planned and waymarked by the Forestry Commission, who own the land. Their route shows off some of the wood's flora and archaelogical remains. It follows mainly gravel tracks, grass rides and narrow paths through woods that are partly ancient and partly planted with conifers. Woodland glades provide patches of sunlight, and a newly planted avenue of native trees adds interest.

Signs of many of Hampshire's ancient settlements have been lost due to intensive farming, so less disturbed areas like ancient woods, such as Micheldever which was probably established in Saxon times, have assumed special importance. In fact this site is considered so important that it is now protected by law. It contains a number of Roman and medieval remains, some of which can be seen along the route.

The walk is also a wildlife trail, and areas along the way have been opened up to provide wildflower glades and to entice butterflies. Micheldever Wood is specially worth a visit in early May, when bluebells cover the ground with a carpet of rich blue for as far as you can see. In July sunshine, the glades are a mass of fluttering and feeding butterflies.

Set off from the car park by the path to the right of the information board. Turn immediately right and then left, following the blue-banded posts. Continue along this path bordered by beech trees, past one of the opened-out glades until reaching a T-junction. Turn right here, following the blue marker Ⓐ.

Ignore paths to the right and the left and continue straight on out into the open. On reaching the gravel track, turn left. At this point you are in the centre of an Iron Age 'banjo'. This settlement, shaped like a banjo, was in use around 2,300 years ago and contained a few wooden buildings surrounded by a ditch. Signs of the ditch are still evident.

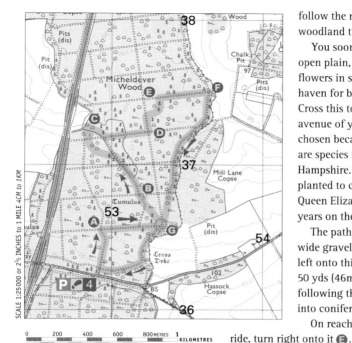

SCALE 1:25000 or 2½ INCHES to 1 MILE 4CM to 1KM

0 200 400 600 800 METRES 1 KILOMETRES
0 200 400 600 YARDS ½ MILES

follow the narrow woodland track.

You soon reach an open plain, rich in wild flowers in summer and a haven for butterflies. Cross this to pass up an avenue of young trees, chosen because they are species native to Hampshire. These were planted to commemorate Queen Elizabeth II's forty years on the throne.

The path then meets a wide gravel track. Turn left onto this **D** and after 50 yds (46m) turn right, following the blue marker into conifer woodland.

On reaching a grass ride, turn right onto it **E**.

Keep your eyes open for the small and slender roe deer and the even smaller muntjac, which are not much bigger than a hare and have tiny spike-like antlers. Both can be seen in these woods crossing a ride or standing, staring from between the trees. Just before the end of the ride, bear right onto a path close to the woodland edge **F**.

The route passes a number of glades where scrub has been cut back to promote woodland flowers and native tree growth.

Continue straight on walking down a natural, narrow hollow, cross another small path and continue ahead, following the blue marker.

Bear right at the end to walk into the banjo, visited near to the start of the walk. This is entered from the same point used by the early settlers. Then, this time, turn left to walk down the gravel track **G** and finally leave this path to turn left back into the car park at the starting point. ●

Pass the blue marker on the right, and soon there is another on the left. Take the narrow path beside this and bear right by the next blue marker **B**. This follows an overgrown ride. Straight ahead, at the end of the ride, is a burial mound, a Bronze Age barrow that is 4500 years old.

Continue round to the left of the barrow, cross a wide grass ride and follow a path straight ahead into the wood. Following blue marker-posts, turn left by the boundary banks sign, which highlights a bank that was built to enclose farmed areas. The way-marked route goes into oak woodland, turning left and then right. It then crosses a path, and a sign calls attention to a fossilised landscape. There is a ditch and bank on the right. The noise of traffic at this point shows how close the M3 motorway is.

On reaching a second Bronze Age barrow, turn right by the sign **C** and

Knightwood Oak and New Forest reptiliary

Start	Millyford Bridge, New Forest; off A35, through Emery Down and turn left at New Forest Inn
Distance	3¼ miles (5.2km)
Approximate time	2 hours
Parking	Forestry Commission Millyford Bridge car park
Refreshments	None
Ordnance Survey maps	Landranger 195 (Bournemouth & Purbeck) and Outdoor Leisure 22 (New Forest)

This short walk visits three of the New Forest's best-known sites. From the car park it crosses a typical forest road, bordered by old and ornamental trees, to pass the Portuguese fireplace. In the 1914–18 war this was part of the cookhouse of a Portuguese army camp with troops living in huts nearby. The walk then takes a woodland route to Holiday Hill Reptiliary where examples of all the New Forest's reptiles can be seen. Passing over a small heath, the route then visits the Knightwood Oak, at 300 years old one of the most ancient trees in the New Forest.

Leave Millyford Bridge car park by going back onto the road and turning right. Almost immediately, on the opposite side of the road there is a grassed area. Walk to the right of it to visit the Portuguese fireplace. During the First World War, Portuguese troops were stationed in the New Forest to help produce vitally important timber. There was a great shortage of local manpower at the time as most forest workers were doing military service. To ensure that meals were cooked in the traditional way, troops constructed this fireplace. It now stands as a memorial to their assistance.

Continue ahead along the wide grass verge at the side of the road for a short distance until a five-bar gate can be seen on the left. Turn left and go through the gate into the inclosure **A**.

Follow the gravel track ahead. Soon it divides, take the left-hand gravel track and continue ahead, ignoring minor paths to right and left, until a gate bars the way ahead. Go through this gate, and the reptiliary can be seen ahead.

Large open-air enclosures hold all the native reptiles and amphibians found in the New Forest: grass snake, adder, slow worm, smooth snake plus sand and common lizard, newt, common toad and frog. All reptile numbers have declined in Britain, due mainly to loss of habitat. Smooth snake and sand lizard are now found almost nowhere else in Britain except Dorset and the New Forest. Apart from providing an opportunity for visitors to view some of these fascinating and shy creatures, the reptiliary breeds rarer reptiles for release back into the forest.

Go through the gate beside the keeper's cottage, out of the reptiliary and down the gravel drive. Turn right in front of the cottage by a no-parking sign to take a narrow grass path that heads for a lone pine tree on the heath the house faces **B**.

The path zigzags through the heather and then widens out to follow the right-hand side of Warwick Slade Heath. Continue along the path which heads for the fence and road beyond. Just before reaching the fence bear right over a footbridge **C**.

Follow the path through the bracken where it bears right, then left. A path comes in from the left, followed by another from the right. When a further path comes in from the left, bear right to head for an inclosure gate. Go through the gate and follow the wide grass ride ahead through the trees. This soon meets a narrow gravel path. Bear right onto this. Ahead, in a fenced area, can be seen the Knightwood Oak.

This pollarded oak tree is over 300 years old. At the time when it was young most trees in the New Forest were cut back to produce numbers of young branches probably used for fuel and charcoal. This resulted in huge trunks and short trees that took up a large expanse of ground space, so in 1698 William III brought in an act forbidding pollarding. This helps in determining the age of trees as most old pollarded oaks and beech in the New Forest are likely to have been planted before this act came into force. The Knightwood Oak is now surrounded by eighteen young oak trees planted to commemorate the Queen's visit in 1979. These trees represent the visits, from William I onwards, of eighteen reigning monarchs to the New Forest.

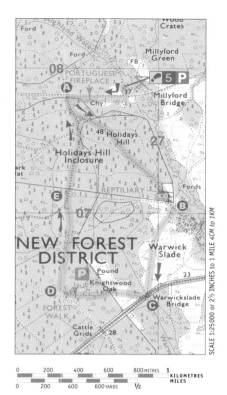

SCALE 1:25000 or 2½ INCHES to 1 MILE 4CM to 1KM

Go back along the gravel path to see two young, labelled oak trees presented by the Queen and the Duke of Edinburgh, then follow the path into the adjoining car park. At the entrance, turn right onto the tarmac road, then almost immediately turn right again onto a path by a fallen beech tree that leads back into the woodland **D**. Follow this wide path bordered by old wellingtonias, giant conifers easily recognised by their cork-like bark. The path goes uphill, eventually meeting a gravel track. Turn right onto this **E**.

Follow this gravel track ahead, ignoring other paths to right and left, for just over ½ mile (800m) until it leaves the inclosure through the gate where you originally entered it. Then walk along the wide grass verge beside the road back into the car park on the left. ●

Busketts Lawn Inclosure

Start	Woodlands. Leave A35 just west of Ashurst, following Woodlands signpost
Distance	3¾ miles (6km)
Approximate time	About 2 hours
Parking	Forestry Commission's Busketts Wood car park
Refreshments	Pubs and cafés at Ashurst and Cadnam
Ordnance Survey maps	Landranger 196 (Solent & the Isle of Wight) and Outdoor Leisure 22 (New Forest)

This walk shows the other side of the New Forest in its role as a working forest. This easy walk goes, for most of its way, through a conifer plantation of straight rides and gravel tracks. The trees, packed close together, are persuaded to grow tall and straight but little grows beneath them. However, a mass of tiny paths wind their way below the trees to show that one group of animals, the deer, enjoy the peace these areas, almost impassable to humans, provide. Grass rides criss-cross the gravel tracks, and this walk follows one of these rides which runs almost from one side of the inclosure to the other. The grass paths can become muddy in wet weather, so waterproof footwear is recommended.

There have been times in the New Forest's history when the fear of ancient woodlands of oak, beech and holly being felled to be replaced by regimented rows of conifers have come close to realisation. Now the forest is cared for by the New Forest Committee which meets regularly and includes members of the Forestry Commission, who manage it on a day-to-day basis, and representatives of the Commoners and naturalist bodies, who together ensure a balance is maintained. The New Forest is nothing like as important for its timber production as the huge plantations of Scotland and Wales but just over 54 per cent of trees in the inclosures are conifers, and around 2000 large lorry loads of timber are felled each year.

Start the walk by passing the wooden barrier to take a gravel track up towards

Grass rides criss-cross gravel tracks

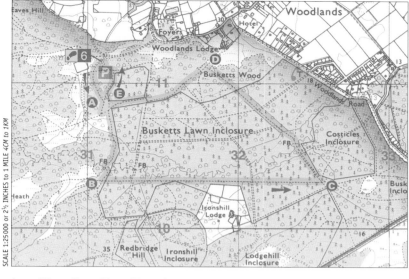

SCALE 1:25000 or 2½ INCHES to 1 MILE 4CM to 1KM

```
0    200   400   600   800 METRES  1
                                   KILOMETRES
                                   MILES
0    200   400   600 YARDS   ½
```

the cricket pavilion. Then follow a now narrow path behind the cricket pavilion, bearing left through the trees. It continues just inside the wood, with heath to the right until it reaches an inclosure fence. Bear right here to follow the path alongside the fence Ⓐ.

The grass path then crosses a narrow ditch and goes back into the trees. Carry straight on, ignoring smaller paths off. Cross a small stream by footbridge and turn left to enter the enclosure through a gate Ⓑ.

Follow the long grass ride ahead through the plantation. It crosses two gravel tracks. To the right are fields and Ironshill Lodge. Just south of the house is Ironshill Inclosure. It is said that Charles II gave all the wood in this inclosure and two others to Winifred Wells, a lady of his court, and intended to give her more until the Lord Treasurer put a stop to it! At the third gravel drive, turn left onto it Ⓒ.

Stacks of timber left at the side of the track are sprayed with a number and initials which refer to the buyer. When the wide track splits, go straight ahead.

The path crosses the dark and twisting Bartley Water by footbridge. *Bart*, the word for 'birch' in Old English, and *ley*, meaning 'wood', point to an original route through birch woods. Ignore a track to the right and continue ahead. When this track divides again, go straight ahead ignoring the track to the left. When the gravel track bears right, go straight ahead up a grass ride.

Leave the enclosure at the end of the ride over a stile. Ignore narrower tracks to the right and left and continue ahead. The track divides to come together again on the other side of trees then comes out into the open by a small pond. At the pond take a path to the left past a burnt tree stump Ⓓ.

The path bears right, then left and soon meets the inclosure edge to run alongside the fence. Cross a path that goes into the inclosure. When you reach the inclosure fence corner, go straight ahead past a tree to see two paths off to the right that leave from the same point. Take the second of these Ⓔ to pass old inclosure fence posts.

At first the other path runs parallel with this one on the right. Ignore paths off to the right and enter the car park ahead. ●

Milford on Sea

Start	Milford on Sea village
Distance	3½ miles (5.6km)
Approximate time	2 hours
Parking	Milford on Sea village car park
Refreshments	Pubs, cafés and restaurants in Milford on Sea
Ordnance Survey maps	Landrangers 195 (Bournemouth & Purbeck) and 196 (Solent & the Isle of Wight) and Outdoor Leisure 22 (New Forest)

The first part of this short walk takes a cliff path above a pebble beach and provides striking views across the Solent to the Isle of Wight and the Needles, which rise from the sea at its western end. The route then turns inland over a small common to follow the woodland course of the Dane stream towards the sea. Although surrounded by houses, the Pleasure Gardens and the stream that runs through it are a quiet retreat full of the song of birds. The path only leaves the stream side to visit Milford on Sea's Norman church from which it returns via the green, the centre point of this village, back into the car park.

The village of Milford on Sea, lies not so much beside open sea as at the entrance to the Solent. From Stone Age implements found close by, it appears that this area has been home to Man for many thousands of years. A mill here and Milford's original church were mentioned in William I's 'Domesday Book'. The village began a period of expansion in the 19th century, and it was at this time that the Pleasure Gardens were planned. Now many of the Victorian cliff-side houses have been replaced by blocks of modern flats.

The Norman All Saints' Church is well worth a visit, and for this reason the route of the walk runs through the churchyard. The tower is 12th century and houses eight bells: faith, hope, love, peace, joy, liberty, patience and victory. Chambers, beneath the lean-to roofs once provided sleeping and living accommodation for the monks from Christchurch Priory who served here before the first vicar was installed in 1339.

Leave the car park by the entrance and turn left onto Sea Road. As you would expect, this road takes you to the sea. When you reach the beach, turn right to follow the made-up path behind the beach huts Ⓐ. From here there are good views of the western end of the Isle of Wight and the famous Needles.

Continue to follow the path as it rises to run along the cliff top. In summer the sea is almost always busy with a constant stream of passing yachts and pleasure craft. Large liners, including the *Queen Elizabeth 2*, pass by on their way from Southampton into the English Channel.

The cliff-top gravel track passes in front of a couple of car parks. At the end of the second car park there is a seat shelter, then some steps to the beach on the left, followed by another seat on the right. Soon after this, at a dog litter box, turn right down a narrow grass path that leads to the tarmac cliff road. Cross this road to go down Westminster road opposite B.

When you reach the T-junction at the end of Westminster Road, go straight across Pless Road and through a kissing-gate down a short grass ride. This footpath takes you through a second kissing-gate and across a field. On the far side of the field go through a small gate onto the common and continue up the narrow path between bushes. When you reach open grass turn right down a narrow grass track which leads to a second area of open grass. Continue ahead to a third area of open grass. Here a seat allows you to enjoy the views. Continue ahead downhill along the path through

another narrow passage off the common.

The path then immediately meets a T-junction with a narrow gravel track. Turn right onto this. Ignore a path on the right and bear left, continuing along the same path. When the path divides take the left-hand fork, ignoring other paths joining it, and continue straight on. The path soon runs alongside the Dane stream which joins the sea beyond Milford village. At a T-junction with a bridge on your left, turn left over the bridge and continue to follow the path with the stream now on your right-hand side. The path soon comes out onto a road C. Cross the road to continue along the footpath with the stream again on your left-hand side.

Newly built houses stretch along the opposite bank of the stream. When you reach a path to the left and a bridge over the stream, take this path D. A recently constructed lake is on the left, which moorhens and mallard have already made their home. On reaching a tarmac lane, turn right onto it and then almost immediately left to follow a footpath through a kissing-gate and up a tarmaced path between houses E.

When you reach a road, cross it and continue up the path, again between houses, on the far side. You will notice that you are walking along Love Lane. A kissing-gate at the end takes you into the churchyard. On the opposite side of the churchyard are two gravestones, lying flat and facing north and south, rather than the traditional east and west. It is said that these graves are those of two suicides, and one bears the inscription '... who departed this life ... after witnessing the departure of all most dear to him, of a wife and many daughters, HE DEPARTED HIMSELF on the ...'

The route turns immediately right after entering the churchyard to go down the side and out of it by a kissing-gate onto the road.

On joining the road **F** bear right to follow the line of an old brick wall. You quickly reach a main road; cross this to continue ahead, alongside the village green. At the crossroads at the end of the green, take the road straight ahead, then turn left back into the car park. ●

View of the Needles rocks and lighthouse at the western end of the Isle of Wight, from the cliff top at Milford on Sea

St Cross Hospital to Winchester Cathedral

Start	St Cross village
Distance	4 miles (6.4km)
Approximate time	2½ –3 hours
Parking	In Mead Road, opposite The Bell Inn
Refreshments	Inn in St Cross, and cafés, pubs and restaurants in Winchester
Ordnance Survey maps	Landranger 185 (Winchester & Basingstoke), Explorer 132 (Winchester, New Alresford & East Meon)

This is a walk rich in history that follows the River Itchen and the water meadows from the Hospital of St Cross, founded in 1136, alongside the river. The route then goes through a 14th-century gateway into the City of Winchester, the beautiful Cathedral Close and, via the cathedral and abbey grounds, to Alfred the Great's statue. The walk returns alongside Wolvesey Palace and ruined castle to footpaths through the meadows and then follows St Cross's quiet backroads, lined with Victorian houses, to the entrance of the hospital once more.

The Hospital of St Cross, founded by William the Conqueror's grandson, was built originally for 'Thirteen poor men, feeble and so reduced in strength that they can hardly or with difficulty support themselves without another's aid'. To these in 1445 were added the Almshouses of Noble Poverty for 'those who once had everything handsome about them, but had suffered losses'. The twenty-five Brothers of today still wear the original gowns. Those of the earlier foundation wear black and a silver eight-pointed cross; the later Beaufort Foundation Brothers wear red. In addition to these two foundations, a hundred poor men were fed every day and if, as a wayfarer, you ask for the 'dole' on visiting the hospital, you will

be given a dole of bread and beer. The entrance to these beautiful, mainly 15th-century buildings and chapel is through a gatehouse passed on the walk.

Go across the main St Cross–Winchester road to take the road beside The Bell Inn which leads passed St Cross Hospital. Just after passing the hospital entrance take the footpath to the river, then cross a footbridge and turn left to follow the river into Winchester **Ⓐ**.

The path ends at Garnia Road. Turn right onto this, cross the river bridge and, immediately after the bridge, turn left onto the riverside path **Ⓑ**.

Across the water are the playing-fields of Winchester College. It was built in the 14th century by William of Wykeham, who also built New College,

Oxford. For 500 years Winchester College has been regarded as one of the country's most renowned schools. Continue by the river, passing the college buildings on the opposite side. At the end of the path, and straight ahead of you, is New Hall. This is the college's concert hall. Turn right here and then at the end of the gravel track, turn left onto the road, following signs to the college and cathedral  C.

Straight ahead of you is the Bishop's Palace. Turn left down a barriered road. You pass the college and then the headmaster's house on your left. Next to this, and marked by a plaque is No 8 Kingsgate Street, the house where Jane Austen died. She is buried in Winchester Cathedral. At the end, turn right under the arch of Kingsgate itself. This is a 14th-century gateway in the city walls. Winchester was England's Anglo-Saxon capital, only being superseded by London in the reign of Edward I in the late Middle Ages. Above Kingsgate is a tiny church, St Swithin's upon Kingsgate, which spans the arch

Winchester Cathedral shows architectural styles from massive Norman to graceful Perpendicular

and is worth a visit. Winchester's east and north gates also had churches over them but they were demolished together with the gates in the late 18th century.

Turn right, through a second archway into Cathedral Close. Cheyney Court, formerly part of the bishop's court house, is on the right, and the cathedral is on the left. Winchester Cathedral was mainly built between 1079 and 1410, and the last major architectural work took place between 1500 and 1530. At the beginning of the 20th century it was discovered that the foundations at the east end were subsiding and would need underpinning. As this part of the cathedral was built on what had been a marsh, the water table was so high that the only way the work could be done was to employ a deep-sea diver! The diver, William Walker, worked for five years, spending six hours a day under up to 20ft (6m) of muddy water until almost the whole cathedral had been underpinned. The cathedral is entered around the left-hand end. To continue the walk, go down the close toward the cathedral. On the right a series of arches are all that is left of the Priory of St Swithin's built in the 10th century to house monks of the Benedictine order. Go through an arch on the right after passing the arches D.

Follow the flagstoned path straight ahead along the side of the cathedral. At the end of this path is a gate. This is thought to be the side entrance through which Nell Gwyn slipped into the cathedral when Charles II was in Winchester. As his mistress she was barred from being part of the royal party.

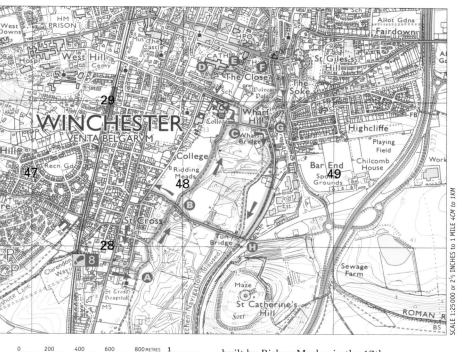

SCALE 1:25 000 or 2½ INCHES to 1 MILE 4CM to 1KM

Turn left through the archway on your left. When you reach the street, turn right and in 20 yds (18m) turn left and go up an alley at the end of the car park, then right into Abbey Grounds **E**.

On the left is Mayor's House, the official residence of the mayor. Winchester's mayoralty is the oldest in the country but the present house dates mainly from the 18th century. Turn right, then left and go across the garden and through the wrought-iron gate out of the abbey grounds. Ahead is a statue of Alfred the Great, king from 871–894, he kept his court at Wolvesey in Winchester.

Turn right onto the road. The old city mill is on the left of the road by the bridge. Turn right just before the bridge over the river **F**, down some steps, then follow the path alongside the river. From the riverside soon bear right to follow the side of a high wall on the right which surrounds Wolvesey Palace,

built by Bishop Morley in the 17th century. The route takes you past the entrance to the ruin of Wolvesey Castle, where the historic English Chronicle was begun by Alfred the Great. It is open to the public.

On arriving back at the street barrier passed earlier in the walk, turn left and retrace your steps down this quiet road. Turn left at the end, alongside the stream, and go over the bridge. Where the road bends sharply to the left, turn right up a private road **G** to pass the college boathouses on the right.

The road soon becomes a gravel track, and where this ends take the footpath signposted on the left. The path runs between hedges, eventually reaching Garnia Road. Turn right on to this **H**, over the canal bridge. Continue along Garnia Road until, at a T-junction, it meets Kingsgate Road. Turn left onto Kingsgate Road. When the road bears right, go straight ahead down St Fath's Road until you arrive back at St Cross Hospital. ●

Queen Elizabeth Country Park

Start	Queen Elizabeth Country Park, off A3 south of Petersfield
Distance	4¼ miles (6.8km). Extension up Butser Hill 4½ miles (7.2km)
Approximate time	2½ hours or 5 hours with the extension
Parking	Park Centre (there is a charge)
Refreshments	Café at the centre
Ordnance Survey maps	Landranger 197 (Chichester & the Downs), Explorer 120 (Chichester, South Harting & Selsey)

This walk is divided into two parts as both sections start from the Park Centre. Although starting from the same point, each short walk is entirely different. The first walk through Queen Elizabeth Forest is, as the name suggests, mainly a woodland walk along gravel tracks through areas of beech and conifers, finally descending to the centre again down steps cut out of the wooded hillside. The second part is across open downland with a stiff climb (for Hampshire) up the South Downs' highest hill to provide the reward of a stunning vista in every direction, including views of the English Channel. Each section would be ideal for a half-day walk, returning to the centre for a café meal or picnic before following the alternative route.

Queen Elizabeth Country Park provides a wealth of activities to appeal to families and includes a shop, café and toilets. A range of special waymarked trails include a teddy bear trail, a space trail and a woodland walk. There are facilities for pony trekking, and the routes include a mountain bike track. Butser Hill is used for grass skiing, paragliding, hang-gliding and radio-controlled model gliders. However the Butser Hill sports are restricted to members of local organisations. The hill is also popular for kite flying.

The walk through Queen Elizabeth Forest begins by following the road around the side of the centre, passing a pond, then a grass picnic area on the left. When the road takes a sharp bend left, go straight ahead up the wide gravel track instead Ⓐ , passing a car-parking area.

Continue on the gravel track, around a single-bar gate. After reaching a barbecue area on the right, the track soon divides; take the right-hand track. This goes downhill, providing views ahead and to the right of typical chalk downland. Pass a wooden five-bar gate and, just before meeting a tarmac road, turn right, following a footpath sign, over a stile **B**.

The path goes diagonally across a field towards trees between two fields. A small wooden gate then takes you through into the next field, and the path follows the left-hand side of a line of trees that acts as a divider between fields. It then leads through a small kissing-gate into the wood.

When you reach a gravel track, turn left onto it and continue straight ahead along this wide track. Narrow paths off the track to right and left point to the presence of deer. A horse route crosses the track; continue ahead until the track meets a partly tarmac road **C**.

Turn right up this road which soon becomes a gravel track and provides good views to the left. Passing tracks to the right and left, a wide grass track beside a pond soon goes off to the right; take this **D**. A fire break in the trees allows a view of the sea.

Cross a bridleway and follow a yellow arrow down a narrow track into the trees. Wooden steps take you downhill where the path is surrounded by ancient yew trees. Continue to follow the yellow arrows and track which winds its way along the wooded hillside. It then bears right to go down steps in the hillside to the gravel track below. Turn right onto the gravel track, then turn left onto the tarmac road to return to the centre.

To take the extension to Butser Hill leave by a signposted path to the left along the wooded hillside above the car

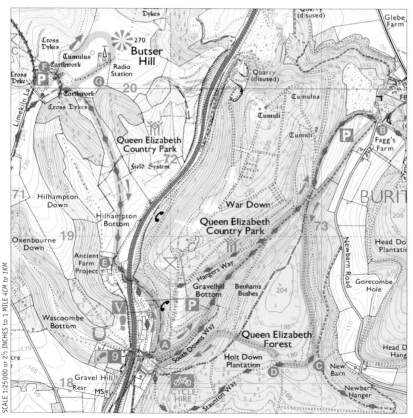

park. This runs parallel with the car park towards the exit. When the path reaches the tarmac road at the entrance to the park bear right to follow the footpath through the underpass. Cross the road on the other side of the underpass and follow the South Downs footpath sign .

Take a narrow gravel path through a swing gate and turn right to walk down the side of the field. Banks can be seen that define the boundaries of the fields of early settlers. Stone Age flint tools have been discovered on Butser Hill. On the eastern slopes there are signs of Bronze Age Man in the form of burial mounds and cross-dykes. Follow bridle-path signs and bear left uphill towards the radio mast between two clumps of trees. This steep hill is used for grass skiing on Sundays. As you reach the top of the hill stop and look back, the views are magnificent. Wild flowers clothe the slopes of Butser Hill in summer.

Go through the small wooden gate ahead and continue climbing with the

Queen Elizabeth Country Park provides special trails for all age groups

radio mast ahead on your right. Go through a second small gate on the left and head towards the cone-shaped roof of the Butser kiosk, a flint and stone roundhouse. Bear left to go through a small gate, then turn right onto a stepped path to the Hampshire brick and flint kiosk. At the kiosk **F** turn right to go through the small gate beside the tarmac road, then bear left to circle the radio mast. This short, circular hilltop route provides views on all sides of the hill. You first see East Meon village and All Saints' Church, built between 1075 and 1150 by Bishop Walkelin, who was also responsible for the building of Winchester Cathedral. Old Winchester Hill, topped by two radio masts, can also be seen. This is the start point for Walk 25. The white marker halfway round the hilltop is the triangulation pillar showing the height above sea-level and used as a map reference. When you reach the gravel track take this route back towards the kiosk until you see a bridleway sign on your left **G**. Turn left here and join the path you took up the hill to return to the centre. ●

River Itchen

Start	Kings Worthy
Distance	4¾ miles (7.6km). Shorter version 4 miles (6.5km)
Approximate time	3 hours (2½ hours for the shorter route)
Parking	Beside small green by St Mary's Church at Kings Worthy
Refreshments	Pub, Kings Worthy, close to start point; or inns at Easton on the way
Ordnance Survey maps	Landranger 185 (Winchester & Basingstoke), Explorer 132 (Winchester, New Alresford & East Meon)

This walk, which follows part of the Itchen Way, first takes a route upstream through the riverside areas of Abbots Worthy and Martyr Worthy, then crosses the river at Chilland to run downstream via the pretty village of Easton. In the latter stages it runs close to the water and in both directions it takes a route under the M3 motorway and across a bypass.

The River Itchen, almost as well-known a trout river as the Test, rises east of nearby Alresford, and the section covered on this walk was an important route for transporting goods from Winchester and further south as far as Alresford in the Middle Ages.

Start the walk by following the footpath sign away from the church down St Mary's Close. At the end of the close, bear right down the side of a garage. The narrow paved footpath goes between houses to the dual carriageway. This section of road was closed off and used in 1944 as a gathering point for vehicles to be used in the D-day landings.

Go straight across the road (be careful crossing, this is a very busy road), then take the continuation of the footpath on the opposite side of the dual carriageway which runs as a narrow grass path beside reedbeds.

On reaching a narrow tarmac lane at Abbots Worthy, cross this and continue ahead on a footpath through an old kissing-gate into a field. Follow the zigzag grass path through the field alongside a couple of buildings and over a stile at the end of the second building. The path crosses the next field on the diagonal, passing old horse chestnut trees to reach the tarmac road in the opposite corner. The path goes onto the road to bypass a house. At Worthy Park on the opposite side of the road a Saxon burial ground was discovered some years ago and when, not long ago, the M3 was being constructed, evidence of a Saxon riverside settlement was also uncovered.

Cross a stile onto the road and turn right to pass the house. Immediately after the house, turn right again over a stile and into a field Ⓐ. The track follows the right-hand side of the field. Cross the stile at the side of the river and take the underpass below the M3 motorway. The path bears left to run parallel with the line of the road, then continues over a stile and crosses fields to follow a fence on the right beside trees. The river runs to the right, a field away. Cross another stile and continue towards a river bridge. From here there is a view of Easton's old church on the other side of the river. St Mary's was built in the 12th century on the site of an earlier Saxon church. It was extensively restored in 1870.

Cross another stile and a tarmac lane and follow the footpath sign opposite down the side of a cottage garden. This path, fenced on either side, goes along the back of houses, then bears left and then right to run between house gardens, then down steps onto a tarmac lane.

If you wish you can shorten the walk by turning right here to cross the river, then right again into Easton village. In this case take up the route again at **D**.

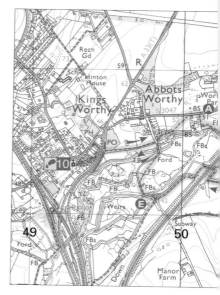

A route across footbridges over the Itchen provides views along this popular trout river

Otherwise turn left onto the lane and walk uphill as far as Martyr Worthy's St Swithun's Church which dates from the 12th century. Turn right opposite the church up a wide gravel track, following the Itchen Way arrow **B**.

Go through a kissing-gate into a field and follow the path with a fence on

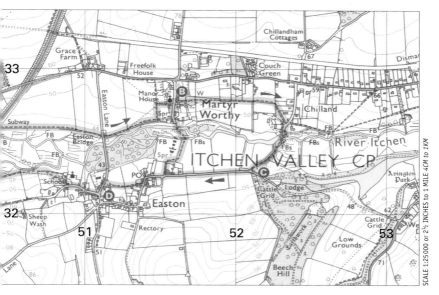

SCALE 1:25 000 or 2½ INCHES to 1 MILE 4CM to 1KM

| 0 | 200 | 400 | 600 | 800 METRES | 1 |
| 0 | 200 | 400 | 600 YARDS | ½ | KILOMETRES MILES |

your left. You can see the river from here. Continue on the path through a second field with a hedge on your left, then through a kissing-gate and over a stile. The path then goes downhill between fences to a tarmac lane. Turn right onto the lane and at the end continue straight ahead over a bridge to cross a small stream. The path then runs down the side of an old barn and crosses the river by footbridge. A gravel path on the other side of the river continues beside reedbeds, then runs over a wide footbridge on to a tarmac lane.

Turn right **C** down this quiet country lane into Easton. This small attractive village has around 450 inhabitants but, as with so many villages, the school, post office and other shops have become private houses. Turn right down a narrow pathway that runs beside the Chestnut Horse pub and over a stile, down the side of a field. The path passes a shed on the left, then continues over a stile and onto a tarmac road. Turn left onto this road and, in about 100 yds (91m), turn right, following a signpost directing you to St Mary's Church **D**.

Pass the church, then the old school, bear right and then turn left, following the footpath sign diagonally across a field. Climb over a stile into a second field and cross this diagonally towards the river. The footpath then follows the river until it turns right and takes you through an underpass below the M3. When the path divides take the right hand track away from the motorway to follow the river, then the road, and go over a stile into a private car park. Cross the car park and take the right-hand public footpath through a garden **E**, across the front of the house, and then over three bridges across the Itchen and its carriers.

After crossing the main part of the river Itchen, pass the Southern Water pumping station and turn left, following the footpath sign. You are now back on the original route of the walk. Follow this track across the dual carriageway, between the houses and back to the start at St Mary's Church.

Southampton Water

Start	Fleetend, between Warsash and Titchfield
Distance	5 miles (8km)
Approximate time	About 3 hours
Parking	Gravel parking area at side of New Road, just off Fleetend Road
Refreshments	Pub at Fleetend, and pubs and cafés in Warsash
Ordnance Survey maps	Landranger 196 (Solent & the Isle of Wight) and Outdoor Leisure 22 (New Forest)

In spite of being located between Southampton and Portsmouth and surrounded by built-up areas, this half-day walk passes few houses and only goes a short distance down a tarmac road before turning onto footpaths and gravel tracks. The path enters the Hook with Warsash Nature Reserve to go through ancient woodland and alongside a steep valley coming out onto Southampton Water. Here faced by fascinating industrial views of the giant oil refinery and power station at Fawley, on the opposite side of the Solent, the route takes the Solent Way along the shore, eventually turning inland and returning on field footpaths. Waterproof footwear is recommended after rain as the gravel track can become pitted with puddles.

Go back to the start of this no-through road and turn right into Fleetend Road. The road soon takes a sharp bend left. Cross the road bridge and then at the bend take the signposted footpath on the right **A**.

This narrow path goes uphill between fences and then meets a gravel track. Turn right onto the gravel track. When the track divides continue straight ahead, ignoring the left-hand turn. When the gravel track bears left take a narrow footpath on the right down the outside of a field fence **B**.

Soon there is a crossing of tracks; continue straight ahead into the nature reserve. The track immediately divides. Take the right-hand track alongside old oak and yew trees and a deep valley on the right. When the track splits and a left-hand track enters playing fields, ignore this and continue through the woodland. The path leaves the nature reserve to meet a gravel track. Bear right to go downhill on this gravel track. At a tarmac road, cross this to follow the footpath sign opposite down a gravel track **C**.

Passing houses on the left, the path again enters the nature reserve over a stile. Follow the path with reedbeds on the right. Here there are splendid views of Hamble and the river where much of the television series *Howard's Way* was shot. On reaching Southampton Water, turn left along the Solent Way by the shore **D**.

From the pebble beach there is a panoramic view of tall chimneys across

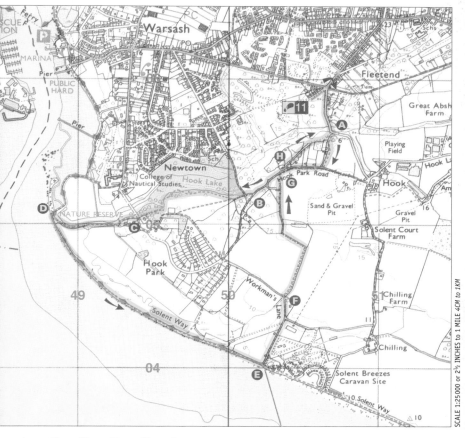

```
0    200   400   600   800 METRES   1
                                       KILOMETRES
                                       MILES
0    200   400   600 YARDS      ½
```

the channel. The oil refinery at Fawley
appears as a group of slim chimneys.
To the left of this, the closer and larger
chimney belongs to Fawley Power
Station and, to the left again, a small
round stone building is Calshot Castle
with the coastguard radar station next
to it. Calshot Castle, which, like Hurst
Castle is positioned at the end of a spit,
was built by Henry VIII in the 16th
century to defend the Solent. The Isle of
Wight soon comes into sight. The view
is of Cowes, the island's leading sailing
centre and renowned throughout the
world for the international races that
occur there during Cowes Week every
August. It was at Cowes, also a
shipbuilding centre, that the first

flying machines were produced, and
Southampton Water became the main
leaving point from which commercial
flying boats once departed on journeys
to places like South Africa.

Continue along the shore for just
under 1½ miles (2.4km). On reaching a
large pond and a house, turn left over a
stile and up the public footpath just
before the garden **E**.

Follow a wide gravel track until it
turns sharp right then go straight ahead
here over a stile to follow a narrower
grassy track. In a short distance a footpath sign points right into a field **F**.

Follow the hedge on the right-hand
side around the field edge, then follow
the fence on the following side left until
you reach a stile. Cross the stile and
walk along the path with a fence
running along the right-hand side

towards a row of cottages. Cross a further four stiles, passing the side of the cottages. When the path reaches a wide gravel track, turn right onto it **G**. Pass a house on the left and, immediately after this, turn left up a track, then bear round to the right to continue on a path that runs down the backs of gardens **H**. The track, narrowing to a small grass path, continues straight ahead, over a concrete stile. When the path reaches the tarmac road, turn left to go over the bridge and back up Fleetend Road into New Road.

●

An evening view shows the chimneys of industrial Fawley across Southampton Water

Meeting of the rivers Anton and Test

Start	Just south of Fullerton off the A3057 Stockbridge to Andover road
Distance	5½ miles (8.9km)
Approximate time	3½ hours
Parking	HCC Westdown car park, just off the A3057 at the Chilbolton turn-off
Refreshments	Inn on the River Test close by on the A3057, at Chilbolton or at Wherwell
Ordnance Survey maps	Landranger 185 (Winchester & Basingstoke), Explorer 131 (Romsey, Andover & Test Valley)

This walk is designed for those who enjoy strolling through undulating farmland and alongside crystal-clear running water. It passes through the valleys of two of Hampshire's best-known chalk rivers. At first following the route of a disused railway line, the walk then crosses the main road to go by Fullerton Mill, set aside a striking millpond on the River Anton, before following the Anton valley through farmland. The route then crosses the river to rise over Red Hill on the far side and drop into the Test valley at the beginning of the village of Wherwell. Here the route crosses the River Test and then meanders back along a part of Hampshire County Council's Test Way, across Chilbolton Common and back to West Down.

The River Test is probably Britain's most renowned fly-fishing river for trout. The sparklingly clear water allows views of fine flecked and spotted specimens on this walk. The River Anton runs into the Test, close to the start of the walk. It is beside the Anton at Fullerton that the remains of a Roman villa have been discovered, and a section of the mosaic floor now decorates the hall of a local house. Fields beside the river here were once water-meadows, and the sluice gates are still evident. An operator, known as a 'drowner', flooded the riverside meadows in winter. This kept the ground temperature up and provided earlier spring grazing the following year.

Leave the car-parking area and return to the Chilbolton road. Cross this and follow the Test Way sign down onto the disused railway line. This was the Andover–Romsey line. As you pass a railway bridge on your left, take a look at the interesting brickwork construction. On crossing the river look out for the working watermill just to the right of the bridge. Follow the track, which

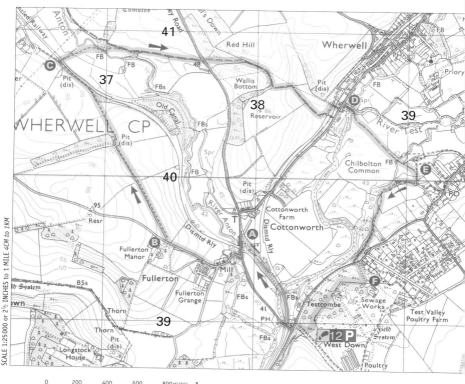

along the cart track that runs at the side of the field, through a space in the hedge at the end and continue straight ahead on the path running down the left-hand side of the following field. Then follow the signposted path across the centre of a field. Many fields in Hampshire have an area of tall maize growing along an edge or in a corner. This is left as cover for pheasants. Pass the water trough in the field centre and, on reaching a cart track that runs alongside the end of the field, turn left onto it. After about 200 yds (180m) turn right, following a signposted footpath through a kissing-gate **C**.

In this area the watermeadow sluices mentioned earlier can be seen. Turn left to cross the river at a footbridge, then turn right through a metal field gate and follow the path along the side of a field. When you reach a tarmac road, cross it onto the bridleway immediately opposite. The path runs up Red Hill, leaving the Anton valley. It then bears

again crosses the Test and then runs alongside Fullerton Junction where the line once divided to run to Whitchurch in one direction and Romsey in the other. Here the remains of a goods siding and the station can be seen on the left. At the main tarmac road, turn left to cross the bridge **A**.

Keep well in as this is a busy road. Just after the bridge, turn right onto the Longstock road. You cannot miss the picture-postcard view of Fullerton Mill on your left. Bear right when the road divides and continue uphill between high banks. At the first entrance to Fullerton Manor turn right opposite, up a gravel track and into a field **B**.

From here there are wide views of the Anton valley and a radio telescope at the Radio and Space Field Station at Chilbolton Down. You may also be lucky enough to see roe deer. Continue right to follow a fence, then left to run uphill again, then finally turns right between hedges.

On reaching the top of the hill Chilbolton village and church and the Test valley can be seen ahead. Turn left here and continue to follow the track downhill. Near the bottom one sees a disused railway bridge, turn left at the waymark and climb a small bank into the field. Follow the curve of the field round the hedge-line and turn right in front of a waymarked stile to go down a set of steps to the road.

The small overgrown copse on the right may still contain some exotic pheasants. The male Lady Amherst's pheasant is dark green and crimson with a black and white tail.

Turn left on the road towards Wherwell village and then, in about 50 yds (46m), follow the Test Way sign and turn right up a bridleway at the end of the garden of a thatched cottage **D**. The priory at Wherwell, close by on the river, stands on the site of an earlier abbey founded in the 10th century by Elfrida. It is said that after her husband, King Edgar, died, she murdered his son. To make amends she built the abbey and ended her life in penance. The priory is the site for another interesting local legend. A tree in the centre of the lawn was blown down, and a man's body was found buried beneath the roots and covered by a hurdle. It is also said that a great treasure is buried here but that sudden death will be the reward for anyone who tries to recover it!

Footbridges take you across the Test River and a carrier of the Test. The path crosses Chilbolton Common. On meeting a gravel track, turn right **E**. Alternatively, if you want to visit the Bishop's Mitre pub, turn left into Chilbolton.

Follow Test Way signs over a cattle-grid and through a kissing-gate onto playing-fields. Keep to the right of the playing-fields, then bear right on the far side down a grass path that runs between two fences. This follows the river and passes private ornamental water gardens on the right. The path then arrives at a small green with a seat and then a tarmac road. Turn left onto the road and then almost immediately right, following the green Test Way arrow onto a concrete path that leads onto West Down **F**.

Take the grassy footpath that runs uphill and to the right off the concrete track onto the down. At the top of the hill take a right-hand path and then bear right again when the path divides and the left-hand track goes into the trees. The path continues along the side of the hill, crossing another track. Take a right-hand fork again when the track divides and follow it down a steep bank, crossing a wider track. On reaching the tarmac road, turn left and you are back in the car park. ●

Alongside the crystal-clear running water of a Hampshire chalk river

Holmsley old railway and Whitten Pond

Start	Holmsley, New Forest; west of A35 and south of Burley
Distance	5¼ miles (8.4km). Shorter version 3½ miles (5.5km)
Approximate time	3 hours (2¼ hours for shorter route)
Parking	Forestry Commission Holmsley car park
Refreshments	Tearooms and pub at Burley
Ordnance Survey maps	Landranger 195 (Bournemouth & Purbeck) and Outdoor Leisure 22 (New Forest)

This walk begins on Holmsley Ridge, an area of high heathland with views over the local New Forest. It looks spectacular in August when the heather is in bloom to clothe the rounded hills with a carpet of rich purple. The path then drops down to Whitten Bottom and sparkling Whitten Pond. Here, during the summer, the water is topped with wild white waterlilies. Surrounded by green lawn on three sides and thick bushes of gorse splattered with butter-yellow flowers at one end, this is a popular spot with picnickers. The path returns along the route of a disused railway line to visit the old station building – now popular tearooms. A shorter route omits the visit to the tearooms and returns to the car park from point Ⓓ. Waterproof footwear is recommended after a spell of wet weather.

Once Holmsley Station was the end of the line. At that time it was called Christchurch Road, and horse-drawn carriages took passengers on to Christchurch and Bournemouth. Later, the line was extended to Ringwood, and the present Bournemouth line – which had previously been stopped by land-owners who refused permission for the route – was finally opened. The platform at Holmsley can still be seen on the walk, as can a number of crossing places and the remains of old railway buildings.

Leave the car park by the entrance, turning left onto the road and then almost immediately right onto a gravel track on the opposite side of the road. Pass the car barrier and follow the track across heath. When the gravel track bears left towards a five-bar gate, bear right up a narrower earth and grass path Ⓐ.

The track follows the right-hand side of a gravel pit. Where the track divides, ignore the left-hand fork and continue straight ahead. The path goes downhill towards two ponds. Follow the path towards the left-hand side of the larger pond. To cross the stream that enters the pond here it is necessary to walk up its side away from the pond until it is

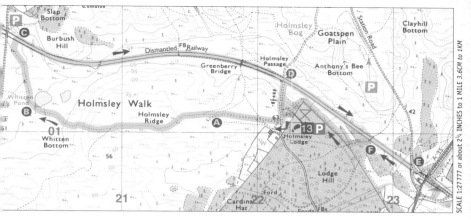

SCALE 1:27 777 or about 2¼ INCHES to 1 MILE 3.6CM to 1KM

0	200	400	600	800 METRES	1
					KILOMETRES
0	200	400	600 YARDS	½	MILES

narrow enough to step across. On reaching the Whitten Pond sign, take the right-hand path away from it **B**. This runs parallel with the road towards trees. When the track divides take the right-hand fork on a less well-defined earth track. You soon reach a shallow bank that runs along the side of the disused railway line. Cross this and turn right to follow the route of the railway **C**.

Walk along the old railway line for about 1½ miles (2.4km). The sunny banks appeal to basking snakes and lizards as well as rabbits whose warrens can be seen along the route. The track crosses a tarmac lane **D**.

Here those wishing to do only the shorter version of the walk can turn right to go up the road back to the car park.

The dismantled Brockenhurst–Ringwood railway line

Cross the road to carry on along the railway line. Soon you cross a wooden bridge and the disused platform of the station can be seen on the right. A fence bars the way ahead. Go towards this, then bear right on reaching it, to go over a stile in the fence onto the road. Holmsley tearooms are on the opposite side of the road **E**. Turn right onto the road and immediately left at the entrance.

Return following the same route along the railway line at first, passing the platform and crossing the bridge. After following marshy ground on either side, the track comes out of the trees into the open. Here, on the left, an inclosure gate can be seen. Go down the railway bank to cross a sleeper bridge, then take the narrow path that bears right **F**. The path snakes through heather and bog myrtle, known as Sweet Gale locally, to reach the inclosure fence. Turn right alongside the fence, following a wide grass ride. On coming to the corner of the fence, turn left to follow the second side of the inclosure into the car park.

The bank is fairly steep at **F**. If you prefer, continue along the old railway line back to the road, then turn left up the road back into the car park. ●

HOLMSLEY OLD RAILWAY AND WHITTEN POND ● 43

Pennington Marshes

Start	Harbour, Keyhaven
Distance	6 miles (9.7km)
Approximate time	3 hours
Parking	Small free parking area by the harbour wall. Alternatively use the official car park (free in winter)
Refreshments	Pubs in Keyhaven and Pennington
Ordnance Survey maps	Landranger 196 (Solent & the Isle of Wight) and Outdoor Leisure 22 (New Forest)

The route of this mainly waterside walk runs through Pennington Marshes with the Solent to one side and both salt and freshwater marshes to the other. Paths are flat and in the main well surfaced and dry, but along short lengths waterproof footwear is advisable.

Pennington marshes are a nature reserve run by Hampshire County Council and are part of a Site of Special Scientific Interest. The marshes are important as a stopping-off point for migrating birds in spring and autumn. They are also important as feeding grounds for winter visitors escaping the extreme cold of their far-northern breeding grounds. One regular visitor from the Arctic is the brent goose which all but died out in the 1930s but whose numbers have now recovered well. Rarer, avocet, arctic skua, snow bunting

Keyhaven harbour, a centre for sailing

and osprey have been seen. The marsh is also, with the Beaulieu River estuary, one of the major breeding sites on the south coast of England for common, sandwich and little terns.

Follow the tarmac lane that runs beside the inner wall of the harbour away from Keyhaven. Ignore a track to the right and carry straight on to a five-bar gate, going around it. Ignore a tall green metal gate on your left with a footpath sign beside it and continue ahead. Soon the tarmac road becomes a gravel track. On the right the sails of boats can be seen apparently moving across a dry landscape. In fact they are passing along a stretch of the Solent in front of the Isle of Wight.

Walk around a five-bar gate and cross a tarmac road, continuing straight on down the lane ahead. When the road bends left, turn right down a narrow gravel footpath between fences **Ⓐ**.

Go around a further five-bar gate at the end of the path and onto a tarmac lane that bears right. Pass a row of old fishermen's cottages on the left and continue down the lane which bears

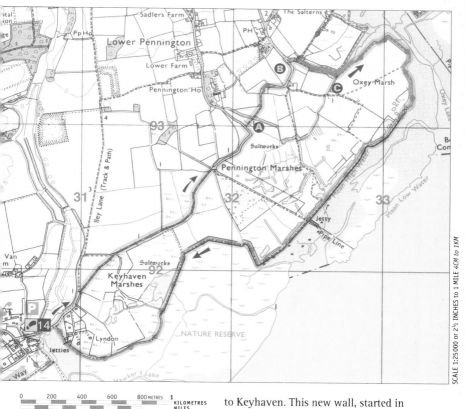

SCALE 1:25000 or 2½ INCHES to 1 MILE *4CM to 1KM*

```
0      200    400    600    800 METRES   1
                                         KILOMETRES
                                         MILES
0      200    400    600 YARDS   ½
```

left. Just before a public footpath sign, turn right onto a narrow gravel track and follow the blue marker signifying the Solent Way **B**.

Bear right at a T-junction on the path to follow a narrow track that leads down the right-hand side of an inlet. On the left the masts of the boats at Lymington Marina are evident, and a chimney in the distance points to the position of Fawley Power Station near Southampton. On reaching the lock that feeds or cuts off water to this inlet, go up the steps beside it and turn right to follow the sea wall **C**.

The shapes of earlier dykes and salt pans can be seen on the right. More information on this salt industry, which thrived for around 600 years, is given under Walk 19.

Continue to follow the sea wall back to Keyhaven. This new wall, started in 1991, is already providing a base for hardy salt surviving plants. It has been designed to include sluices and flaps to allow salt water to pass through to the marshes inside the wall so that plant life and feeding birds will not be affected. The path then follows the shoreline.

From here the lighthouse at Hurst Spit and Hurst Castle can be seen. Like Calshot Castle, Hurst was one of a series of forts built by Henry VIII to defend the coast. Since then it has been used, among other things, as a prison. Its most famous prisoner was Charles I who was held here for a short time before being returned to London for his trial and execution. Follow the path back alongside the harbour.

You can visit Hurst Castle by boat or by walking along the pebble beach. It is about 6 miles (9.5km) there and back. A boat leaves the harbour regularly for Hurst Castle in summer. ●

Beaulieu River

Start	Beaulieu village
Distance	5¾ miles (9.3km)
Approximate time	3–3½ hours
Parking	Beaulieu village car park
Refreshments	Pubs and cafés at both Beaulieu and Bucklers Hard
Ordnance Survey maps	Landranger 196 (Solent & the Isle of Wight) and Outdoor Leisure 22 (New Forest)

This delightful walk alongside one of Britain's most unspoilt rivers is a favourite with local people. Historic interest abounds both in the two villages and along the way. Wildlife, specially birds, appreciate the peaceful marshes. The route starts in the lovely old village of Beaulieu and at first follows part of the Solent Way through fields and woodland, then alongside a boat-building yard and the marina into the tiny village of Bucklers Hard. Here the one village street runs up from the river. Its old houses are set alongside a wide gravel track and lawns. No traffic is allowed into the village. The walk returns by the marina to run along the river's edge, joining up with the original route back through the fields into Beaulieu again.

The village of Beaulieu nestles close to the river. Allow time to explore its village streets of mainly 17th-century buildings, erected from local bricks made close to the route of this walk. On the opposite bank of the river stand the ruins of Beaulieu Abbey, the Cistercian monastery, founded by King John in 1204, and Palace House, the present home of the 3rd Baron Montagu of Beaulieu. Palace House and gardens, the ruins of the monastery and the National Motor Museum are all open to the public. Why not set aside time to visit these too?

Leave the car park, walking back towards the entrance, then take the gravel track to the right of it that leads between buildings into the village street. Follow the footpath sign on the opposite side of the street, which leads up a gravel track that again runs between buildings. Take the path through a kissing-gate onto a small green. Cross this green diagonally to the right-hand corner and go over the stile onto a gravel track. Turn right along the track **A**, crossing a stile to the right of a field gate, and follow the wide gravel track ahead. Dogs should be kept on the lead here.

There is a good view from this track of the Beaulieu River across a field to the left. The river was a vital thorough-fare to the monks of Beaulieu Abbey who exported wool and timber and imported luxury foods like sugar and spices. Continue along the track over a second stile beside a cattle-grid. The path then goes down the side of a

SCALE 1:25000 or 2½ INCHES to 1 MILE 4CM to 1KM

0	200	400	600	800 METRES	1
					KILOMETRES
					MILES
0	200	400	600 YARDS	½	

second field. Follow the blue arrow and narrowing track along the side of a river inlet through a valley, then up a hill, through another gate and down the side of a further field. Pass the cottage at the end of the field, go through the gate and onto a vehicle track **B**.

At the beginning of the track, on the left, is a large, tall-chimnied old building now turned into a dwelling. This is one of a number of buildings that were part of a thriving brick-making industry in the 18th century. The trade continued until the 1930s, when the distinctive white as well as red handmade bricks were outpriced by mass-produced alternatives. Many

houses in the surrounding area show their lineage in the use of these decorative old bricks.

Another industry that flourished beside this river until the early 19th century was salt production.

Continue ahead on the vehicle track as it bears right and at this point follow the green footpath sign to Bucklers Hard. Ignore a second wide track that comes in from the left and bear right instead, then almost immediately left onto a narrow gravel path, following the green arrow **C**. Continue straight along this path for some distance. The wood, Keeping Copse, was planted partly to produce timber for use by the shipbuilders of Bucklers Hard, while other trees were coppiced to produce a number of thin stems for the local

This river was used to depict the 16th-century Thames in the film A Man for All Seasons

charcoal trade. On reaching a car park on the left, go through the gate ahead and, bearing right, walk along the wide vehicle track. On the left at Keeping Marsh are man-made mudflats produced when the river was dredged to deepen the channel for the marina at Bucklers Hard. Rich in food, these mudflats are popular with wading birds.

Follow the track, passing a modern shipbuilding yard on the left, into the car park. To the left of the car park is a narrow gravel track, signposted River-side Walk. Take this path, which leads down to the river and by the side of the marina, into Bucklers Hard .

Many early fighting ships were built at Bucklers Hard, including Nelson's HMS *Agamemnon*, launched in 1781. Nelson served in her in the Mediter-ranean from 1793 to 1796. In more modern times the village was the home port for Sir Francis Chichester's *Gipsy Moth IV*, which became famous when he sailed her round the world in 1966. The Maritime Museum to the left at the top of the village street provides much more visual information on Bucklers Hard and includes interiors of cottages that show life in the village during the 18th century. The village,

intended to be much larger, was built by the 2nd Duke of Montagu around 1724. After loosing a fortune in the West Indies, only the 80ft- (24m) wide main street was completed.

Leave the village and return along the same route to Keeping Marsh and the car park at the start of Keeping Copse. Here follow the 'Riverside Walk' sign to the right around the back of the car park .

The gravel path continues along the riverbank with spectacular views along the river and across to the opposite bank with its imposing houses. Finally the path curves left away from the river and joins the original gravel track through the wood. Turn right onto this and retrace your earlier steps towards Beaulieu. On going through the gate onto the wide gravel track, ignore the stile and path into the village street originally followed and instead continue straight ahead . This gravel track leads past the fire station and the side of the Montagu Arms Hotel. Turn left on reaching the road and, keeping the mill-pond on your right, turn left back into the car park. A common site is a large black cormorant that often sits atop a wooden post in the centre of the pond. ●

Standing Hat, New Forest

Start	Standing Hat, Brockenhurst. Up gravel track behind Balmer Lawn Hotel
Distance	6 miles (9.7km)
Approximate time	3 hours
Parking	Forestry Commission Standing Hat car park
Refreshments	Cafés, pubs and restaurants in Brockenhurst
Ordnance Survey maps	Landranger 196 (Solent & the Isle of Wight) and Outdoor Leisure 22 (New Forest)

This woodland walk in the main follows gravel tracks and wide grass rides. The grass rides can be muddy in wet weather. The route reaches the main railway line through the forest. Here wide grass lawns on either side of the track allow easy walking, and a pond provides extra interest. Crossing to the south side of the line, the path follows the railway for a short distance then returns as a narrower grass path through woodland to cross the railway again. The last part of the route is along a gravel track back to the car park. A mixture of conifers and deciduous trees is encountered along the way, and the rusty shades of oak and beech make this a beautiful autumn walk.

These woods are home to the tiny roe deer and the tall, slender fallow, the most common deer of the New Forest. Woodpeckers of all three types can be seen here and, as dusk approaches, a tawny owl may fly silently overhead, calling to its youngsters, or a woodcock may fly low across your path.

You may also catch a glimpse of a grass snake as it swims through a stream.

Leave the car park to go through the side gate beside large double gates into the inclosure and take the left-hand gravel track. Follow this track as it curves sharply left. When the track bends left again, two grass rides go off to the right. Take the first of these grass rides Ⓐ, ignoring the ride with a notice 'No cars'.

Cross another grass ride and continue straight ahead. The path goes downhill, across a footbridge and then uphill again on the other side. When you reach a gravel track, cross it to continue on the grass ride straight ahead. On reaching another grass ride bear slightly right onto it. When the ride meets a gravel track, turn left onto it Ⓑ.

Go through a gate, cross a wide avenue of grass and through a second gate. These wide strips of grass are found in many parts of the forest and usually indicate the line of an underground pipe. Continue along the gravel track for about ¾ mile (1.2km). Along the sides you will notice what look like organised heaps of pine needles. These are the carefully constructed nests of wood ants. Holes in the nest surface point to raids by hungry green wood-peckers whose main food this is.

Where the track takes a sharp left-hand bend there is a five-way crossing **C**. From here carry on almost straight ahead by taking the second right. Continue, ignore a cross track and, on reaching a gravel track, turn left onto it **D**.

Continue along the gravel track, ignoring the right turn to a railway bridge. When the track begins to bear left, turn right onto a grass ride **E**. At the end of this ride it is necessary to climb over a wooden barrier, where you turn right to walk on the wide grass area that runs alongside the railway **F**. If wet underfoot, the driest path may be found against the tree line.

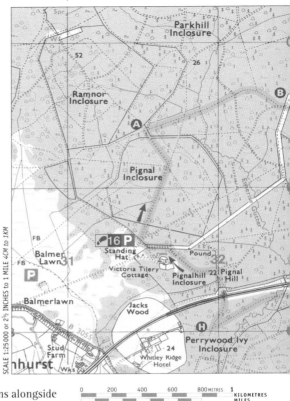

SCALE 1:25000 or 2½ INCHES to 1 MILE 4CM to 1KM

| 0 | 200 | 400 | 600 | 800 METRES | 1 |
| 0 | 200 | 400 | 600 YARDS | ½ |

KILOMETRES
MILES

This railway line is the main track from London Waterloo to Dorchester. It was constructed in the mid 19th century, and not far from here stand old beech trees carved with the date 1854 and a caricature of a man with a long nose. It is said that these carvings were done by workers constructing the railway and that the figure is the un-popular railway construction manager. When the railway opened, the fencing to keep the deer and stock off the track was not finished, so men were employed along the unfenced sections to warn the driver if an animal had strayed onto the line.

On the right is a pond that was dug by the railway to provide water for the steam engines. Now the surface glows with white waterlily flowers in summer, and train passengers are often provided with a glimpse of a heron, ponies or deer at the pond-side as their train speeds by.

On reaching a gravel track, turn left to cross a bridge over the railway. Where the ramp levels out, turn right onto a grassy plain **G** and head for a line of conifers bordering the railway. Walk parallel with these and go through a small copse to emerge onto a wide expanse. The railway fence is on your right and an inclosure fence is on the left. The track is ill-defined but continue straight on to cross a foot-bridge. The railway is on the right, woods on the left.

Some years ago a postman returning to the sorting office in Brockenhurst

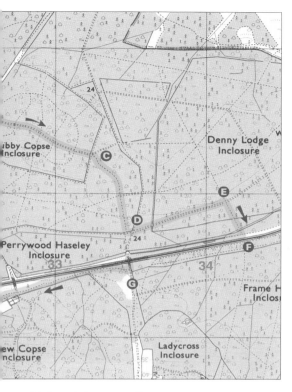

them is still sometimes seen.

Cross the track between a lone forest house on the left and a bridge spanning the railway on the right, keeping close to the railway fence. When you see a tunnel under the railway on the right, bear left and enter an inclosure through a single wicket-gate on the right. Continue over a footbridge and on until you meet a four-way crossing **H**, where you turn hard right.

The path slopes gently up to a gate in front of a railway bridge. Go through the gate, over the bridge and through a five-bar gate. Carry straight on across a track – the surface is now gravel – and head for another five-bar gate. Go through the gate and turn left. The car park at the start of the walk is now in sight at the end of the track. ●

told the unbelieving staff that he had encountered a wallaby on his route! This strange story appears to be true. In a storm a few years before, two wallabies escaped from the field adjoining a house close by, and one of

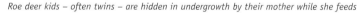

Roe deer kids – often twins – are hidden in undergrowth by their mother while she feeds

Selborne and Noar Hill

Start	Selborne village
Distance	5¼ miles (8.4km)
Approximate time	3–3½ hours
Parking	Selborne village car park
Refreshments	Pubs, tearooms and hotel in Selborne
Ordnance Survey maps	Landranger 186 (Aldershot & Guildford), Explorer 133 (Haslemere & Petersfield)

After leaving this renowned Hampshire village, the route of the walk soon leads away from the busy through-road and up into woodland to the nature reserve on Noar Hill. Continuing around the hillside, the path provides panoramic views of the surrounding farmland. It then descends through fields and along an ancient track before rising again to Selborne Hill. The final descent is made along a narrow zigzag path back into Selborne. It is well worth allowing time at the beginning or end of the walk to wander through the village and visit the museums and church.

Selborne was made famous by the eminent naturalist Gilbert White who was born here in his grandfather's vicarage in 1720. He spent most of his life in the village studying and writing about natural history and wrote the book which has made him inter-nationally well-known, *The Natural History and Antiquities of Selborne.* His old home is now a museum and stands opposite the church of St Mary, built around 1180. A yew in the churchyard made news when it was blown down in the gales of 1990. By then it was around 1,400 years old and 26ft (7.9m) in girth. Unwilling to loose this important part of their history the villagers had the tree replanted. It is too early yet to tell whether it is regrowing successfully.

It is appropriate that this walk runs first through Noar Hill's ancient chalk quarries, now a nature reserve renowned for its wild flowers and attendant butterflies in summer. Thirty-five species of butterfly have been recorded here. It is also a good site for cowslips, and eleven species of orchid grow here.

Much of the local countryside is now in the hands of the National Trust, including Selborne Common, and the zigzag path cut out of the hillside by which the walk returns to Selborne was made by Gilbert White and his brother in 1753.

Leave the car park by the entrance, down the side of the Selborne Arms pub, onto the main road that runs through the village. Turn right along the road. A monkey-puzzle tree on the far side of the road is made more noticeable because of the bat boxes that surround the trunk. You soon pass the Romany Folklore Museum. Continue down the hill until reaching the Gilbert White drinking trough on the right-

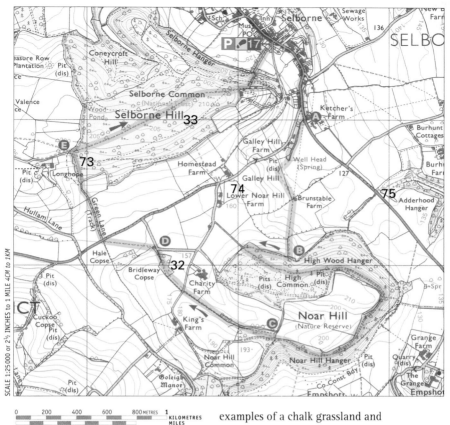

0	200	400	600	800 METRES	1

KILOMETRES
MILES

0	200	400	600 YARDS	½

hand side of the road. Just after this, turn right and go over a stile and onto a footpath across a field **Ⓐ**.

The path goes through a gap in the hedge, then turns left down the side of the hedge. Cross the stile at the end, then continue to follow the path slightly to the right and uphill. Cross a further stile and follow the footpath sign straight ahead. As you climb the hill you start to get some good views over the surrounding countryside. Climb a further stile, turn right onto the bridleway **Ⓑ**, then keep to the footpath that runs parallel with the field-edge fence.

On reaching a wider gravel track, turn left uphill, then bear right to go through a gate onto the nature reserve. This reserve, considered one of the best examples of a chalk grassland and scrub mosaic, is in the care of Hampshire Wildlife Trust. The gravel track becomes a grass ride. When the track divides, take the left-hand fork into the wood alongside a fence. Go over a stile beside a metal gate and then take the left-hand narrow grass path downhill. On reaching a wider track turn right uphill. The path continues along the side of the hill with wonderful views across the Hampshire country-side. When the path meets a bridleway turn right onto this.

Ignore the Hangers Way sign off to the left and continue along the path straight ahead. At a meeting of paths, take the one most straight ahead which bears slightly to the right and uphill **Ⓒ**. Continue through the wood until the path divides, bear right here and, on reaching a field, cross the stile into it and walk along the right-hand side of the field until reaching a tarmac road. Cross the road and continue along the bridleway straight ahead. After passing alongside the field, the path enters woodland and then reaches another tarmac road. Turn left onto this road and walk down the hill for 20 yds (18m) before turning left to follow a footpath sign into the field **D**.

The path crosses the middle of the field. At the far side, go through a small gate and straight across a tarmac road to follow the bridleway up Green Lane. This, probably ancient, track takes you up Selborne Hill to reach Selborne Common, owned by the National Trust. Ignore the path signposted Selborne

Church and instead go straight on, then bear right soon after onto the 'Selborne via pipeline' footpath **E**.

On coming out of the trees, a path joins from the left; continue ahead. Ignore paths from the right and left until reaching a seat on the left. It is well worth taking a short rest here to enjoy the view over Selborne village. Finally turn left in front of the seat, then right to take Gilbert White's narrow gravel track and steps down the hillside. On reaching the bottom of the hill, go through the kissing-gate and follow the path down into Selborne.

The car park is on the left at the bottom of the path. ●

The decorative Gilbert White fountain at Selborne forms a landmark on this walk

Greywell and the Basingstoke Canal

Start	Swingbridge, North Warnborough; close to M3, exit 5
Distance	6¼ miles (10.1km)
Approximate time	4½ hours
Parking	Parking bays close to canal swing-bridge, off Bidden Road
Refreshments	In Greywell and North Warnborough
Ordnance Survey maps	Landranger 186 (Aldershot & Guildford), Explorer 144 (Basingstoke, Alton & Whitchurch)

This walk blends historic interest and an area rich in nature with tranquil and beautiful surroundings. The walk starts along a quiet country lane with footbridges aside two deep fords. A footpath soon leads off the lane to run through a belt of bushes. Waterproof footwear is essential here in wet weather. The woodland that follows is of native trees, mainly oak, holly and hazel, and part of it is a Site of Special Scientific Interest due to its rich variety of flora. Please keep to the route of the walk as this area is protected. A gravel track leads over the canal, and the path continues across farmland, then through the small, attractive village of Greywell where it joins the canal at the entrance to the longest canal tunnel in Britain. From there the route follows the canal, past the ruins of Odiham Castle, back to the swing-bridge starting point. Dogs need to be kept on the lead for part of this walk.

The Basingstoke canal was built in 1792 and remained in use until 1937. The section covered on this walk is at present a quiet backwater, popular with wildlife. In fact the Basingstoke canal is Britain's finest water area for aquatic plants, and more species have been recorded here than anywhere else in the country. The Greywell Tunnel is important also as Britain's largest winter roost of bats. There is much pressure on Hampshire County Council to open up more of the canal to motor craft but at present this section is only used by some canoes and a few long-boats, hired out from close to the swing-bridge.

Begin the walk by crossing the swing-bridge over the canal. Continue straight ahead up a narrow tarmac lane, over bridges at the side of two fords. Just over the second ford, turn left between houses and stables following a footpath sign.

After passing the last house, bear right, then left down a narrow path between bushes. This area can be

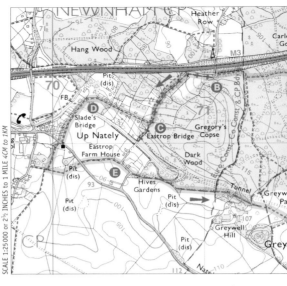

muddy in wet weather, and the path divides periodically in an endeavour to avoid the muddiest areas, soon coming together again. Signs of deer show up in their slots, prints, in the mud. On reaching a tarmac road, cross it to follow the footpath over a stile. Bear left towards a house. You soon come out onto the end of a further tarmac road, cross this and take the path to the right of a house and past a metal gate, following a footpath sign **A**.

Continue into Butter Wood – a conservation area. Where the track forks, bear left, following the yellow arrow. Where it divides again after 50 yds (46m), bear right. Cross a track and continue ahead, following the yellow arrow. After passing through an open area, the track meets up with one from the left and continues ahead as a wide track to pass pheasant-feeding stations. These metal drums allow a controlled amount of grain to fall on the ground and so provide food for hand-reared young birds when they are first released prior to the shooting season. You pass huts on the right and reach a wide ride. Bear right here and then almost immediately left, following the wide gravel track to pass out of the conservation area **B**.

Bear left along a wide track. Ignore a track to the left and continue straight on downhill. This cart track can be muddy but a path above it follows its route. After passing a house and stables on the right, at the end of a field, a narrow track goes off to the right. Take this **C**.

This path goes through scrub, then opens out into a wide gravel track.

Continue down the track with houses on both sides. Two old arches, one on either side of the lane are all that is left of a tiny railway that took bricks made in nearby brickworks to be transported on the canal. Cross the canal by a bridge **D**. A short detour on the tow-path to the right goes down to a narrow concrete bridge that temporarily replaces an older and unusual rising bridge. This is where docks led off the canal, and the wreck of the *Seagull* can be seen in the water.

Return to the track which goes uphill after the canal crossing to reach a tarmac road opposite St Stephen's Church Up Nately. Cross the road to follow the footpath at the end of the churchyard over a stile. Keeping the field fence on the right, follow round two sides of the field and over a stile into the field on the left. Cross this field to a stile next to the gate and onto a tarmac road. The route crosses the road and, following a footpath sign, goes over a stile and straight ahead. Keep the fence ahead on the left. Go over a second stile and follow another path

through the hedge, down a short length of track onto a tarmac road. Turn right down the lane **E**.

After 200 yds the road bears right. Here take the bridleway straight ahead. Ignore a right-of-way to the left and continue straight on. Cross a wider track and keep straight on, following the bridleway. The track eventually leads to a metal field gate. Take the small gate at the side and go ahead uphill, between two large oak trees, across the field. Impressive Greywell Hill House is on the right, and the village street, known as The Street, is below. The manor was acquired by the first Lord Dorchester, who was the first Governor General of Canada in 1786, and it has remained with the family since that time.

On the top of the hill a footpath sign with a yellow arrow points the way ahead to a stile in the far corner of the field. The path continues between fences to a tarmac road. Turn right onto the road and then take the road almost immediately to the left **F**. Alternatively, go straight ahead down The Street to visit the Fox and Goose pub. Greywell no longer has any shops.

Having turned the corner on the route and passed a house on the corner, turn left onto a footpath signed Basingstoke Canal and Greywell Tunnel. Cross over a stile, then follow the route along the backs of gardens. The canal can soon be seen on the right. Turn right onto the towpath **G**.

Greywell Tunnel is on the right. The tunnel is ³/₄ mile (1.2km) long but is not at present navigable, having collapsed in three places in 1932. There is controversy between those who want to rebuild it to make the canal wholly navigable again and the naturalists who wish to preserve what is now one of our most important bat colonies.

Many water birds can be seen on the canal here, moorhen, coot, grebe and some unusual ducks. Ignore a footpath sign to the left and continue along the towpath, past a boom across the river. The canal then crosses the river White-water, seen on the left. The river goes under the canal in pipes.

The path then passes Odiham or King John's Castle on the left. Built about 1207, this small fortress was constructed as a resting place where the king could stop and hunt on journeys from Windsor to Winchester. In 1216 the castle was besieged by the French for fifteen days. These invading French were so impressed by the courage of those defending the castle that they allowed them to surrender yet retain their freedom. When the defenders marched out of the castle, to the stunned surprise of the French, it was seen that it had been held by only thirteen men. Scotland's King David was imprisoned here from 1347 to 1357. When the canal was built the engineers cut through the outer baileys and moat so little is now left but the ruins of one keep.

Ignore a footpath sign on the left and follow the towpath back to the swing-bridge.

●

Lymington saltmarshes and estuary

Start	Lymington
Distance	6¼ miles (10.1km)
Approximate time	2½–3 hours
Parking	Town car park, New Street
Refreshments	Pub on route or restaurants, hotels, pubs and cafés in Lymington
Ordnance Survey maps	Landranger 196 (Solent & the Isle of Wight) and Outdoor Leisure 22 (New Forest)

This is a leisurely walk along some of Lymington's most attractive roads and down surprisingly quiet country lanes to a 17th-century inn. The route then follows the sea wall back into Lymington, passing the site of the old saltworks, Lymington's major industry from the 12th to the 19th century. The past is soon set aside by the modern marina with its tinkling metal masts, which provides most of today's revenue to this pretty waterside town. Lymington is one of the Solent's major yachting centres. The route then winds its way via The Quay up the old cobbled street of Quay Hill back into High Street.

Lymington, positioned at the lowest point where the Lymington River could be forded, has probably been the site of a settlement from early times. Certainly Bronze Age implements have been found at nearby Buckland Rings. The main market town and port for the New Forest, Lymington has regular ferries which cross to Newport on the Isle of Wight. The High Street is mainly Georgian, to which modern shop-fronts have been added. This leads downhill via an attractive cobbled street to The Quay. Once Lymington's high street had permanent market stalls down its centre and it is still the site of a thriving Saturday market.

Come out of the main car park entrance and turn left up New Street, past the Community Centre. Turn left at the end to reach High Street. Go straight across the road and take Ashley Lane opposite. At Madeira Walk go straight ahead, passing a bike barrier, to go down a tarmac footpath. There is a park on the left. At the end, bear right down Grove Road beside an old brick wall **A**.

On reaching Church Lane, turn left onto it and, at a Y-junction by a pillar-box, bear left down Waterford Lane. This road soon comes to a main road. Cross this to walk down King's Saltern Road opposite. When the road curves to the left, turn right onto a public footpath through the reedbeds **B**.

At the end of the path, turn left onto a narrow tarmac lane. Continue ahead down this quiet lane with wild flowers,

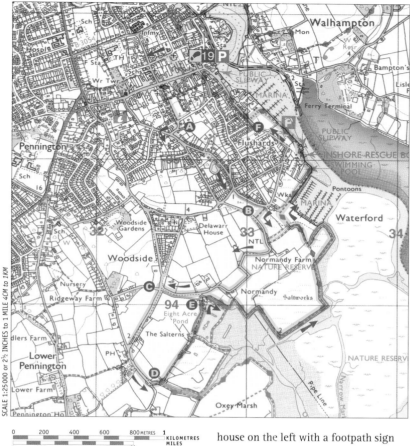

SCALE 1:25 000 or 2½ INCHES to 1 MILE 4CM to 1KM

```
0    200   400   600   800 METRES  1
                                    KILOMETRES
                                    MILES
0    200   400   600 YARDS  ½
```

and bramble and honeysuckle hedges. On reaching a grass triangle with roads to the right and to the left, turn left onto Platoff Road. **C**

Ignore Poles Lane that goes off this immediately to the right and continue ahead until you see the 17th-century Chequers Inn, also on the right. The name comes from the fact that this inn was once the salt exchequer, where tax was collected on the salt produced nearby. There were as many as 163 salt pans around the town in the 18th century, producing 4600 tons of salt between 1724 and 1766.

Continue down the lane that runs alongside the pub until you reach a house on the left with a footpath sign pointing up the drive. Turn left to follow the footpath in front of the house **D**. It soon becomes a narrower gravel track, then widens out again to pass the office of the Hampshire County Council Nature Reserve. The track then becomes a tarmac road to pass a pond on the right. Eight Acre Pond is home to some rare pondlife that mainly lies hidden in the mud, a bristleworm, starlet sea-anemone and the shrimp-like *Gammarus insensibilis*. But you are much more likely, and probably more excited, to see a fishing heron or kingfisher here.

On passing a sailing club and a cottage at the end of the pond, turn right up a track that runs alongside the pond **E**. This soon comes out by the sea, turn left along the sea wall.

The site of some of the old saltworks are on the left. These were made on flat land which was divided by mudbanks into a number of shallow pools. Here the water was left to evaporate. Windmills pumped the water into pans until only brine was left. This then went into boiling houses. Each salt pan made three tons of salt per week.

Go through the kissing-gate onto the marina and bear right to follow the marina edge and then continue along the sea wall. The route takes you past the swimming pool and the Royal Lymington Yacht Club. Follow the path through public gardens, bearing left by the pond to reach the road. Turn right here **F** and walk along the road as far as The Quay.

At the end of The Quay, bear left to go up the narrow cobbled Quay Hill which leads to the bottom of High Street. Go up High Street to the point where the elevated pavement descends to road level. Here turn right into Early Court which leads back into the car park. ●

The old cobbled Quay Hill in Lymington

Brockenhurst old church and Ivy Wood

Start	Ivy Wood; B3055 just south of Brockenhurst
Distance	6¼ miles (10.1km)
Approximate time	3–3½ hours
Parking	Forestry Commission Ivy Wood car park
Refreshments	Pubs, cafés and restaurants at Brockenhurst
Ordnance Survey maps	Landranger 196 (Solent & the Isle of Wight) and Outdoor Leisure 22 (New Forest)

This walk goes via a country lane to Brockenhurst's tiny old historic church. It then passes through a woodland nature reserve out onto farmland and returns through ancient New Forest woodland finally to take a track alongside the Lymington River in Ivy Wood, renowned for its wonderful display of spring flowers – mainly primroses, violets and wood anemones. Some paths may be muddy after wet weather.

Allow extra time on this walk to visit the forest church passed on the route. St Nicholas' Church stands on a mound away from Brockenhurst village and surrounded by fields and forest. It is the oldest church in the New Forest and mentioned in William I's 'Domesday Book'. This small church, with its musicians gallery, has a Norman archway over the south door and tall, narrow 13th-century arches containing later windows of stained glass flowers. In one wall a part of the masonry is very early – from 5th or 6th century.

The walk starts from Ivy Wood car park. Go towards the car park entrance. Just before the entrance, take the narrow grass track off to the left. This descends towards the river and then runs along its side, ending on the road at a crossroads. Turn left here, down a lane signposted Brockenhurst, crossing the river by the bridge **Ⓐ**.

Walk along the side of this country lane for ¾ mile (1.2km). Keep in well as this lane has a number of blind bends. Pass the gatehouse to Brockenhurst Park. The old house, Brockenhurst's manor, was replaced by a modern brick building some years ago, but the original owners, the Morants, have left their mark in large Ms on some of the estate workers' houses; one can be seen opposite the gatehouse. Turn left up a wide gravel track between two houses **Ⓑ**.

At the top of this short track on the right is St Nicholas' Church, and it is well worth taking a slight detour through the churchyard. To the left of the church entrance is a yew tree reputed to be at least 1,000 years old. The graveyard has two memorials of special interest. Brusher Mills, mentioned under Walk 26, is buried here, and his gravestone depicts his colourful life. This Victorian character is seen outside the charcoal burner's hut where he lived for around thirty years, holding a handful of snakes. During his life he caught thousands of snakes in the forest, some of which went to zoos to feed other snakes, and some were sold for their skins or fat. Now numbers are much depleted, and all British snakes are protected by law.

Close to Brusher Mills grave, and on the north side of the churchyard, is a memorial to the New Zealand soldiers who died at a nearby hospital for the seriously wounded during the 1914–18 war. Brockenhurst also had numbers of wounded Indian soldiers quartered there, and one road, Meerut Road, is named in their memory. In the churchyard there is also a bench beautifully carved with animals of The Forest in memory of a local naturalist.

SCALE 1:25000 or 2½ INCHES to 1 MILE 4CM to 1KM

| 0 | 200 | 400 | 600 | 800 METRES | 1 |
| 0 | 200 | 400 | 600 YARDS | ½ | KILOMETRES MILES |

In front of the church the track joins a country lane. Turn left and walk along this lane for a short way until the road bends to the right with farm buildings on the right. Opposite the farm entrance, turn left down a narrow fenced track between two fields **C**.

Shortly, you will see an avenue of trees that runs across the path in each direction. Known locally as the Gallops, this avenue was used for training racehorses. Thatched Cottage, which won a Grand National in the 1950s, was one of a number trained here. This was also the site of the hospital for New Zealand wounded mentioned above. Continue along the track, which enters Roydon Woods, a nature reserve. If you are lucky, you may catch sight of one of the three kinds of deer that can be found in these woods: sika, fallow and roe. The track runs up and down in a gentle switchback through woodland. When the path reaches a T-junction with a gravel track, turn left onto it **D**.

Carry on along this track, disregarding a track that leads to a house on the left,

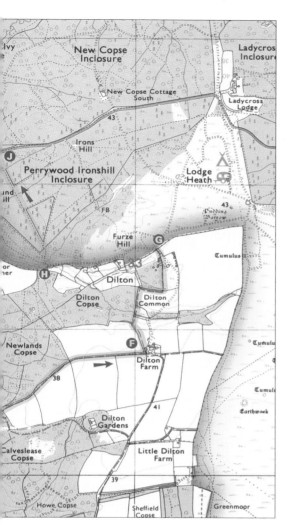

which may be muddy after wet weather. Just before farm buildings on the left, turn left through a gate down a narrow track signed 'bridleway' **F**.

Follow this clearly defined path for some way until you reach a wider made-up track, where you turn left to follow the bridleway sign. You may still see signs that this was once a made-up road, part of Beaulieu Airfield, which was used extensively during the Second World War. Now it has largely returned to the wild. Go through a gate to meet a further wide track. Turn left onto this track **G**, passing houses on your left.

On leaving the houses behind, the track runs downhill. Where two streams meet, ignore the gravel track on the left, cross the smaller stream and turn right on a narrow

and continue downhill. On reaching a gate on the left, recognised by a red-and-white-topped metal post by its side, turn left down this track **E**.

The path passes Roydon Manor on the left, the present home of the Morant family, mentioned earlier. It was also for some years the home of the author and naturalist W H Hudson at the end of the 19th century. He wrote *Hampshire Days* while he was here. The path descends to a bridge crossing the Lymington River then leads away uphill, passing a field on the right. It finally leaves the wood through a five-bar gate to follow a wider gravel farm track with fields on either side,

path uphill through the woods **H**.

Paths may be difficult to identify during some seasons of the year. The path bears left shortly before the remains of a gate into a wide, grassy inclosure. Bear left here and continue to follow a narrow path with woodland, a valley and stream to the left at first. The path then runs parallel to a fence on the left. Just before reaching a tarmac road, a narrow path goes off to the left down the side of a fence. Take this path that runs downhill to the river **J**. Continue following the path upstream along the river until you re-enter Ivy Wood car park. ●

Portsmouth and the Wayfarers' Walk

Start	Purbrook Heath, Purbrook, off A3 north of Portsmouth
Distance	6½ miles (10.5km)
Approximate time	4–4½ hours
Parking	Borough of Havant car park, Purbrook Heath
Refreshments	None
Ordnance Survey maps	Landranger 196 (Solent & the Isle of Wight), Explorer 119 (Meon Valley, Portsmouth, Gosport & Fareham)

This medium length walk follows, in part, an early section of the Wayfarers' Walk. In spite of being little more than a ten-minute drive from the centre of Portsmouth, it goes down quiet country lanes and on field paths through typical Hampshire rolling farmland. In wet weather some areas of the fields can be muddy, specially where cattle stand, so waterproof footwear is advisable.

The route begins by running parallel with the high ridge of Portsdown Hill – 6 miles (9.7km) long. There are six forts built along the length of the ridge, and Fort Widley, the one most obvious from this walk, is halfway along. The forts were erected during Queen Victoria's reign because the country was worried about an invasion from France. The defences included sea forts on the southern side of Portsmouth and these hill forts on the northern side. Lord Palmerston ordered the forts to be built but Gladstone, who was Chancellor at the time, threatened to resign in protest against the idea. It is said that Palmerston told Queen Victoria that it was better to lose Gladstone than Portsmouth! However, the fortifications were never needed and became known as Palmerston's Folly.

Leave the car park by the entrance and turn left up the road. When the road bears sharp right, take a lane off it slightly to the left. Continue straight on past Widley Walk on the left. This country lane goes uphill, passing a small oak copse on the left. It then turns sharp left. Follow the turn and, almost immediately, there is a stile next to a metal field gate on the right. Turn right to cross the stile Ⓐ.

Walk straight ahead with a fence and woodland on your right. To the left is Portsdown Hill and Fort Widley, or rather the surrounding buildings, which can be clearly seen. The fort is built of brick, surrounded by fortifications and a deep ditch on the northern side. This was the side it was designed to defend, and in fact the fort itself is scarcely visible. It contains a labyrinth of underground tunnels used for moving the ammunition.

| 0 | 200 | 400 | 600 | 800 METRES | 1 |
| 0 | 200 | 400 | 600 YARDS | ½ | KILOMETRES MILES |

At the far end of the field, climb over a stile and continue ahead, keeping the fence on your left. Cross the next stile at the end of the fence and head for the farmhouse opposite. Cross the stile next to a gate onto the road and turn right up the road. Just after the farm and a field on the left, turn left over another stile to go into a wood. This cart-track takes you through the wood. The path eventually passes an area of newly planted young trees, and a single yew

tree can be seen ahead at a left-hand bend in the track. Just before this bend, a narrow path goes off to the left, snaking its way to a stream which it crosses via a footbridge and then leads onto a tarmac road. Turn right onto the road **B**.

This lane bears to the right then meets another road at a T-junction. Take this road left. When the road bears left, a footpath crosses it. Turn left here onto the footpath which leads up a wide track **C**.

Follow this track uphill. As well as Fort Widley on the left, HMS *Dryad* can be seen ahead. You are also walking parallel with the line of a Roman road on your left but there is little evidence of its course. The track then turns right and passes farm buildings on the right. At a second group of buildings, follow the footpath sign and a path that runs down the right-hand side of the buildings. The old farm track continues between hedges. When you reach a fence across the track, turn right over a stile .

Follow the fence on your left. At the far end, by a copse, there is a gate on the left into the adjoining field and a stile by the side. Cross the stile and head across the field towards the farm buildings. Go over a stile into a farmyard and turn right down a track that takes you to a lane. Turn left onto the lane. After passing a house on the right, but before a bungalow, turn right, following a footpath sign into a yard .

Head for the gate opposite into a field and go across the middle of the field and over a stile in the hedge opposite, then cross a ditch by footbridge. Follow the line of the hedge on your left until you reach an opening in the hedge. Cross through to the adjoining field and follow the same hedge on the opposite side. On reaching a house, bear left around the garden to go over a stile onto the road. Turn right onto the road, pass the farm and immediately after crossing the river turn right again, then over a stile to follow a Wayfarers' Walk sign along a track with the river on your right .

At the end of the track, turn left to cross a stile, following a Wayfarers' Walk and footpath sign. Cross this field on the diagonal towards a gateway in the right-hand corner. Keeping the wood on your right, follow the side of the wood until you reach a stile on the field corner. Cross it and turn left to follow a path through the wood. On going through newly planted young trees and uphill, you reach a group of conifers on top of the hill. Here paths go to right and left as well as straight ahead. Turn left .

Follow the track through the trees and over a stile into a field. With the wood on your left follow the side of the field, go through an opening into the field on the right and continue ahead, following the hedge on your left. Continue ahead into the next field, still following the track with the hedge on your left. The track continues to metal gates and a stile. Cross the stile onto a road and turn right. Almost immediately there is a footpath sign on your left just beside a farm entrance. Follow the track across the field and through into the next field. It then curves to the right around trees and uphill past newly planted trees. Here the path meets another crossing it. Turn right .

Follow the path alongside the trees and a fence on your right, past a new house. When you reach the road, turn left, and the car park is across the road on the right. ●

A view from Portsdown Hill

Silchester and the Roman town

Start	St Mary the Virgin Church, Silchester
Distance	6¾ miles (10.9km)
Approximate time	4½ hours
Parking	Parking area by St Mary the Virgin Church
Refreshments	In Silchester
Ordnance Survey maps	Landranger 175 (Reading & Windsor), Explorer 159 (Reading, Wokingham & Pangbourne)

A historically fascinating and relatively easy walk; the route starts from Silchester's lovely 12th-century church to follow an old drove track through the centre of what was the Roman town of Calleva, now buried beneath Hampshire farmland. It leaves the site of the town by its west gate and continues through farmland to enter an ancient wood, now a nature reserve, where dogs must be kept on a lead. Here the wide and well-used bridleway can be muddy in wet weather so waterproof footwear is advisable. The route continues across Silchester Common and into the village, passing the tiny museum where more information on the excavations of Calleva can be gained. It then returns alongside the north wall and via the site of the amphitheatre.

The Roman market town of Calleva Atrebatum prospered between around AD 160 and 410 from when it was probably gradually abandoned to lie below the fields until the late 19th century. The town was both an administrative capital and the centre for an agricultural area, shown by the many agricultural tools found on the site. Protected by ramparts and a ditch, the walls, originally up to 22ft (7m) in height, can still be seen. The Romans were not the first people to make Silchester their home. There was a still earlier settlement here, a centre for the Atrebates, a tribe who migrated from northern France in the 1st century BC.

Excavations of the area within the town walls were carried out by the Society of Antiquaries between 1890 and 1909, and from this work a plan of the site was produced. The town was laid out on a rectangular grid pattern and, because the area has never been built over, the ground plan is the most complete of any provincial town in the Roman Empire. After the excavations, the remains were reburied to protect them from both souvenir hunters and natural weathering.

The nature reserve on the route is well known for its flowers and butterflies. Anemones, primroses and violets make the reserve a colourful

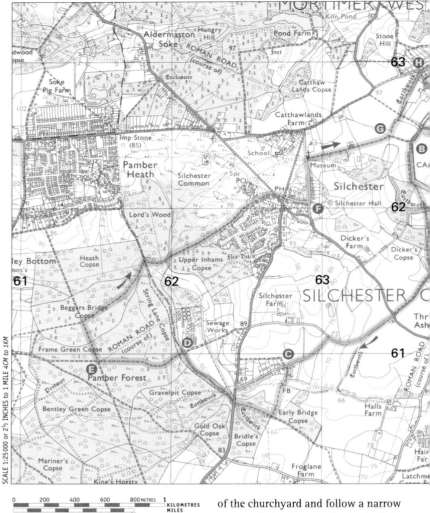

| 0 | 200 | 400 | 600 | 800 METRES | 1 |
| 0 | 200 | 400 | 600 YARDS | ½ |

KILOMETRES
MILES

place to visit in the spring. The tiny museum is open during daylight hours.

When you leave the car park, walk towards the church of St Mary the Virgin and into the churchyard. The little church, situated just inside the Roman wall, was built in the 12th century on the site of two previous Roman temples. It is well worth a visit. Notice the carved dog-tooth ornament in the north porch above the doorway and the door itself and lock, all thought to be original.

Leave by the kissing-gate at the end of the churchyard and follow a narrow grass path that bears right. On the left you can see the line of the old city wall. Go through a small pretty old wrought-iron gate, then bear left through another narrow wooden gate onto a wide farm track **A**.

This track is the old drove. From here, surrounded by the walls, you can see spaces that show the positions of the original town gates. About halfway along the drove is the site of an old Romano-British church hidden beneath the turf. This is said to be the earliest known urban church north of the Alps. The foundations of the town's forum and basilica are also nearby. The track

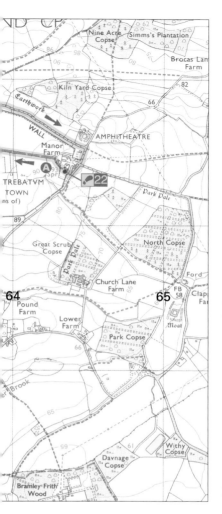

until you pass a line of trees running across the field. Here the fence turns left. Instead, continue straight ahead across the field. On the opposite side, cross the stile and follow the left-hand side of the adjoining field, then cross a stile at the end onto a lane.

Go up Byes Lane opposite. The lane bears left, and a track goes off ahead. Continue along the lane. You soon reach some houses. Just before a house on the left, Little Acre, turn left down a signposted footpath **C**. The path follows the side of the garden, then trees on the left and turns right to cross a bridge over a stream. It then bears left to follow a narrow path through conifer woodland. Follow yellow markers to bear left again around trees. When the path reaches a wide track turn right onto it and continue to follow yellow markers, almost immediately bearing right again to go through the wood.

Continue ahead until you reach a road. Cross this, bearing slightly right to follow a bridleway sign above the Silchester Village sign on the road. This narrow, gravel path goes through ancient woodland. Signs in the form of prints in the mud show there are deer around.

This path, which can be muddy in wet weather, widens out and then follows the edge of the wood.

Cross a main gravel track, then, when you see sewage works through the fence ahead of you, turn left onto a gravel track into the nature reserve **D**. Dogs must be kept on a lead here.

This reserve is well known for its flowers, and some of the rarer butterflies such as purple emperor, white admiral and silver-washed fritillary can all be found here. Ignore two narrow paths which cross the main path and continue ahead. When the track reaches another equal in width, turn right down this wide grass path **E**. Notice the trees

bears left. Just about here was the town's west gate.

Take a kissing-gate on the left **B** following a yellow arrow. The route goes down the left-hand side of a field. The old wall and adjoining ditch run on your left. Go through the kissing-gate beside a metal gate at the end of the fence and follow the short length of track which ends at another kissing-gate. Ahead of you, across the field, you can see yet another kissing-gate. Head towards this and go through it into a narrow wood, also the site of earthworks. Follow the path through another gate out into fields and continue with the fence on your right at this cross-track which are well supplied with bat boxes, easily recognisable from bird boxes as they have a narrow slit entrance in the base. When you again reach a cross-track, turn right onto this, and at a further cross-track, continue ahead, following a bridleway.

Cross a small footbridge over a stream then go over a stile out of the nature reserve. Cross another track and continue ahead, following the footpath sign through Silchester Common. This path crosses a wet area on duckboards then divides. Take the right-hand narrow earth track which follows the line of an enclosure bank and ditch on the right. The path goes uphill. Ignore a path to the left and continue ahead beside the fences of house gardens. When you reach the tarmac road, turn left onto it.

At the end of the road, turn right towards the crossroads and go across the main road to take Whistlers Lane opposite. This gravel road leads to a T-junction with a wider tarmac road, turn left **F**. Bear right soon, to follow the bridleway down the side of the tiny Silchester Museum building, which

provides information on the Roman town and excavations. Go up this gravel track and over the stile at the end. When the path bears slightly right, turn left over a stile to follow a signed footpath **G**.

Go towards the stile ahead but bear right when you reach it to follow the fence on your left as the path has been rerouted. Cross a fence on a path that takes you through a ditch, then over a stile and into a field. Go straight ahead, following a hedge on your left, then through the gateway, following a yellow arrow, and continue ahead, this time with trees and bushes on your right. The hollow on your right is the site of earthworks. Cross the stile onto a tarmac lane and turn right **H**.

This lane takes you alongside Calleva's north wall. Just after the wall turns to the right and away from the lane, you will see two kissing-gates on the left, leading into a field. A short detour takes you through the original entrance into the site of the Roman amphitheatre. Returning to the lane, follow it when it bears round to the right. When a road comes in from the left continue straight ahead back to the church and the car park.   ●

Silchester's 12th-century church stands on the site of two previous Roman temples

River Test near King's Somborne

Start	Horsebridge opposite the John o'Gaunt pub
Distance	7 miles (11.3km)
Approximate time	About 5 hours
Parking	Test Way car park, Horsebridge
Refreshments	In Horsebridge, and Broughton
Ordnance Survey maps	Landranger 185 (Winchester & Basingstoke), Explorer 131 (Romsey, Andover & Test Valley)

This walk is equally rich in historic interest and the beauties of Hampshire's round-hilled chalkland countryside. The route at first follows a disused railway line – a summertime haven for wild flowers and butterflies – and part of the Test Way. Never far from the Test, it then crosses the river in a number of places, providing views of huge silver-flecked trout for which this chalk river is so famous. It turns onto part of the 24-mile- (39km) long Clarendon Way and continues through Houghton village and across farmland. An ancient track crosses the route of an old Roman road, and the path leads back across the river. Finally the path follows another part of the disused railway that passes an old station and signal-box, attractively restored and, together with a row of carriages, used as holiday homes.

Go back to the car park entrance opposite the John o'Gaunt pub and turn left onto the road. Pass a renovated water mill on the right, and soon there is a Test Way Inkpen Beacon sign on the right of the road. Take this path, which follows the route of an old railway line and soon crosses the river. Continue along this path until reaching gates where the Clarendon Way crosses the Test Way. Turn left here onto the Clarendon Way **A**.

The Clarendon Way is another of Hampshire County Council's long-distance paths and runs from Salisbury to Winchester.

Follow the Clarendon Way, which crosses carriers of the river a number of times and eventually reaches a tarmac road at Houghton village. Turn left onto this and follow it past houses until reaching a wooden seat on the right of the road. Turn right up the tarmac road, just beyond the seat, still following the Clarendon Way **B**.

Ignore a footpath sign on the right and continue up the road which soon becomes a farm track. From this track there are good views of the surrounding countryside. It passes a sherpherd's old caravan on the right. This is typical of the caravans once used by shepherds

Horsebridge Mill stands beside the River Test

through the lambing period so that they could remain night and day with their flocks. Follow this track past Hayter's Copse and down the hill where it bends to the right. Leave the track on the corner to go through a gap in the hedge and turn left onto the drove road 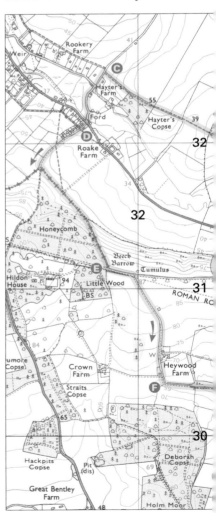 C .

Drove roads are old routes once taken by farmers and local people to drive their animals to market. Keep straight ahead to cross the ford by a wooden bridge onto a narrow lane. If you wish to make a detour into Broughton and a local pub, turn right here and walk ³/₄ mile (1.2km) into the village.

The route of the walk goes straight across the road and up the Hollow D . Tracks or roads named Hollow are often very ancient routes, so called because they have been worn hollow by traffic and rain. This tarmac road passes houses and soon becomes an earth track which goes under a canopy of tree branches. Ignore footpaths to the right and left. On Broughton Hill ahead a Saxon warrior's skeleton, including his blond hair, was uncovered by a ploughman in the 19th century.

When the track splits into three, and a narrow footpath runs straight ahead, turn left and follow the grass track along the field edge and into a windbreak of trees. Walk through this until you reach a tarmac road. Turn left onto the road E .

This road follows the route of a Roman road which once went from Salisbury to Winchester. A burial mound on the left of the road is opposite a road to the right with a cul-de-sac sign. Turn right down this road. When the track bears sharp right at the bottom of a hill, go straight on, following the right-of-way sign. Then go left, through a gateway F .

Follow the wide grass track ahead. Continue ahead, through a gateway and into a milking yard. Go through this and follow the concrete track that goes down to a tarmac road. Turn left onto the road and follow it until you reach houses and a farm drive on the left. Opposite the drive, turn right onto a gravel track between fields .

On the left is Bossington's tiny country church. A hamlet too once stood here but in 1829 was destroyed by the owner of nearby Bossington House.

A field near here is locally known as 'Agincourt'. In 1415, Henry V, on route with his army for Southampton and the Battle of Agincourt, encamped here, unable to cross the Channel because of unfavourable winds.

Go across the bridge over the river. Look to the left where an old thatched fishing hut creates a delightful picture. Then, after crossing a second bridge over the river, bear left across a field towards old willow trees. Here a stile leads onto the disused railway line. Turn left and follow the path. This leads alongside the old signal-box, railway station and carriages, now restored and used as holiday homes. Take the narrow track to the right at the end of the station which leads back into the car park.

SCALE 1:25000 or 2½ INCHES to 1 MILE 4CM to 1KM

Rockbourne and Whitsbury

Start	Rockbourne
Distance	6¾ miles (10.9km)
Approximate time	4½ hours
Parking	Rockbourne Church Hall car park
Refreshments	Inns at Rockbourne and Whitsbury
Ordnance Survey maps	Landranger 184 (Salisbury & the Plain), Outdoor Leisure 22 (New Forest)

Starting in the beautiful village of Rockbourne, this walk goes by the little medieval church which clings to the hillside above the village. It then follows the valley and an avenue of glorious rust-red copper beach into the nearby village of Whitsbury, passing the stud and racing stables that have made this village well known. A bridleway beside the racing stables turns to follow an old track lined with ancient yew trees. The route returns through woodland and rolling fields where there are pleasant views of the surrounding countryside.

Rockbourne's chalk stream, which gave the village its name, runs alongside the road, so the residents of the thatched cottages and Hampshire flint and stone houses reach the road over bridges that span its width. Sadly, the stream is most often dry nowadays. The 16th-century pub, set back from the road with a garden in front, was bought in 1991 by a group of fifteen local people who were keen to preserve its character and keep it a free house. Set some time aside to visit the nearby museum and remains of a large Roman villa. For the opening hours telephone 01725 518541. There is a fee. Come out of the car park and turn right to follow the village street for a short distance. (If you wish to visit the pub, turn left). On reaching the war memorial on the right, take a signposted footpath left off the road that crosses the stream and goes through a gateway. Follow the path by the side of a brick wall, then over a stile and turn left onto a narrow path.

Almost immediately a footpath to the right follows the side of the churchyard; take this path **Ⓐ**.

Cross a stile at the end onto a made-up track and turn left down the track for about 20 yds (18m) through a wicket-gate on your left beside a cattle-grid. Go downhill, through a second wicket-gate and follow down to the farm buildings. Go through the wicket-gate at the bottom and round the side of the barn. At the next finger-post, turn right and follow the track uphill **Ⓑ**.

On reaching a gate alongside a small shed, go through the gate, then alongside rails and through a second, small metal gate to take the path ahead that meanders through a narrow belt of old beech trees between two fields. Continue straight on, through a small gate, eventually walking down an avenue of

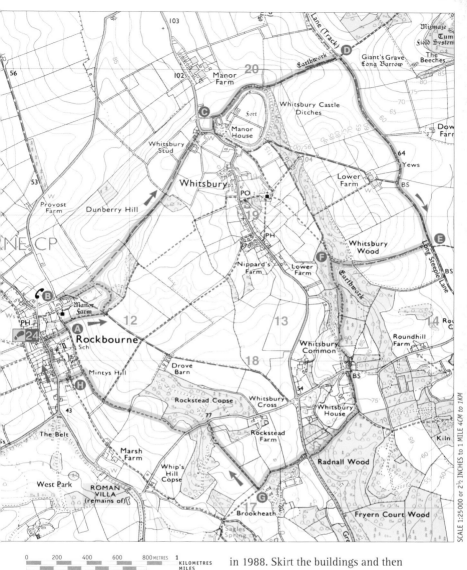

SCALE 1:25 000 or 2½ INCHES to 1 MILE 4CM to 1KM

0	200	400	600	800 METRES	1
					KILOMETRES
					MILES
0	200	400	600 YARDS		½

copper beech. At the end of the avenue the route passes alongside Whitsbury stud, then goes through a gate, beside a row of houses, to meet a tarmac road.

Turn right onto the road then very soon turn left, following the bridleway sign **C**, which goes up the side of the training stables. These stables have trained some well-known racehorses, including Red Rum, and Rhyme and Reason, which won the Grand National

in 1988. Skirt the buildings and then bear left, following the bridleway sign. When the track veers to the left, go straight on alongside a gate, following bridleway signs.

The track goes downhill. At the bottom of the valley there is a T-junction with another track, and a small footpath continues ahead. Turn right onto the track that runs along the bottom of the valley **D**.

This wide and easily followed track continues for some way, often bordered by yew trees. It is said that a route lined

Close to Rockbourne and the route of Walk 24 are the remains of a Roman villa

by yew trees is sure to be an ancient route. Pass a track to Down Farm on the left and continue straight on.

On reaching a bridleway sign and a small wooden gate on the right, turn right through the gate **E** and follow the track that leads uphill beside the field with the fence on the right. Look out here for roe deer. At the top of the field go through the gateway and follow the cart-track into the wood. As you reach the top of the wooded hill a path comes in from the left; take this **F**.

Continue on this path along the top of the hill which passes between two concrete blocks positioned to stop four-wheel drive vehicles using the track. When the path divides, bear right to join a tarmac lane. Turn left along the lane to leave it almost immediately, following a bridleway sign to the left. This path runs between houses and down to another tarmac lane.

Go across the lane to take a narrow bridleway on the opposite side. When this track divides, take the right-hand fork around the back of Whitsbury House. Follow this track until it reaches a road.

Turn right onto the road then, almost immediately, turn left, following the footpath sign up the side of a house.

The narrow track follows the garden edge into woodland and alongside fields. At a T-junction with a gravel track, turn right onto the track **G**.

This leads to a road. Turn left to follow it downhill. Part-way down the hill there is a stile and footpath sign to the right. Take this path across the field, skirting the field edge in the centre section.

There are good views from here. The monument to Sir Eyre Coote points skywards on the left. Lieutenant-General Sir Eyre Coote, born in 1726, gained fame when, as a young army officer in India, he persuaded Robert Clive to attack quickly at the Battle of Plassey. As the British won this battle it made his name. Continue down a narrow track along the side of the next field and then go over a stile onto a wide farm track. Cross the track and go over the stile opposite, following the footpath sign ahead. This newly laid path runs between a fence and hedge. Turn left at the next footpath sign **H**.

Go over a stile and down the right-hand side of the field, then go over a further stile straight ahead. This takes you down a short narrow path onto a wide track that leads to the road. Turn right into the village and church hall car park. ●

Old Winchester Hill and Garden Hill Lane

Start	Car-parking areas off Old Winchester Hill Lane, between East Meon and Meonstoke
Distance	8 miles (12.9km)
Approximate time	4½ hours
Parking	In English Nature car park just off Old Winchester Hill Lane
Refreshments	Pub at Exton, approximately halfway on the route
Ordnance Survey maps	Landranger 185 (Winchester & Basingstoke), Explorer 119 (Meon Valley, Portsmouth, Gosport & Fareham)

This exhilarating walk begins from near the top of Old Winchester Hill, crossing the old hill fort to lead down through fields and then follow the direct route of Garden Hill Lane, a track in a hollow thought to be centuries old. The walk then passes watercress beds on the River Meon into the attractive small village of Exton. It then passes through the neighbouring Meonstoke to return across farmland, where Old Winchester Hill shows the way back. It must be noted, however, that the section between points ⒷⒷ and ⒸⒸ is often impassable after heavy rainfall.

Leave the car park by a small gate beside a five-bar gate. Where the path divides into four tracks, take the grass track on the left, next to the gravel track on the extreme left, and follow this wide grass path along the hillside, with the road on your left.

Looking to the right, the first sight is of Winchester Hill and the bank that surrounds the old Saxon fort on the top. Turn right onto a path beside a gravel track with a field fence on the left. Carved wooden seats are dotted along the route. Go through a swing gate and follow the main path which bears left. Then bear right on a path that goes across the top of the hill, entering the area of the fort between two mounds,

probably the original entrance to the fort Ⓐ. The views from here are spectacular.

When you reach the bank at the far end of the fort, the track divides. Go straight on, taking the left of the two tracks. Cross a stile and follow the path into a copse, then through a swing gate and down the side of a field. The path turns right. When the track turns right into a field, go straight on following the yellow arrow. On coming out of the trees, continue ahead, now following a farm track for about 200 yds (183m). A narrow lane goes off to the left. At the footpath signs, turn left down this lane Ⓑ. This is the start of Garden Hill Lane, the ancient route mentioned earlier.

Continue along it for just over 1 mile (1.6km) during which time the track passes under a disused railway bridge. On reaching a T-junction with a farm track, bear right onto the track and then immediately left down a narrow path between two fences .

This path bears left to cross the river by footbridge and then meets a main tarmac road. Cross the road to go straight ahead, following a lane sign-posted Exton, with watercress beds on your left. When a road comes in from the left, turn down it past the Shoe Inn, which has gardens by the river. Turn right at the T-junction after the pub and follow the road round to the left at the point where a narrower tarmac road goes straight ahead. This lane then bears right. At this point take the footpath that runs down the side of barns on the left.

Go through a kissing-gate. The path then bears left to follow a hedge on the right and passes a lovely old wrought-iron kissing-gate. The river is on the left. Head for the corner of the field at the side of a cottage. Cross the stile in front of the attractive Meonstoke Church of St Andrew and turn left onto the road. The name Meonstoke comes from a tribe of the post-Roman period, the Meonware. When you reach the main road, turn left over the bridge and then take the first road on the right past the village post office.

When this narrow road reaches a T-junction with another tarmac road, turn right onto it. At a second T-junction turn left, pass a cottage on the right and turn right, following a footpath sign at the end of a car-parking area.

The path follows the end of a garden and tennis court. Continue along the path behind houses and over two stiles. After the fourth stile the route follows a fence that sticks out into the field. Cross a fifth stile, then go over a stile, two-thirds down the hedge facing you. Cross the next field, following the same diagonal to go over a stile at the end. The route continues under the disused railway line. Go straight ahead of you, following a path towards the backs of houses with a fence on your left. Cross a stile. The path then bears left to meet a tarmac lane. Go straight across the lane. At the end of a short grass track go over a stile and continue along the side of the field with a fence on the left. Cross another stile and follow the path to a space in the hedge ahead of you. The track follows a fence on the right for a

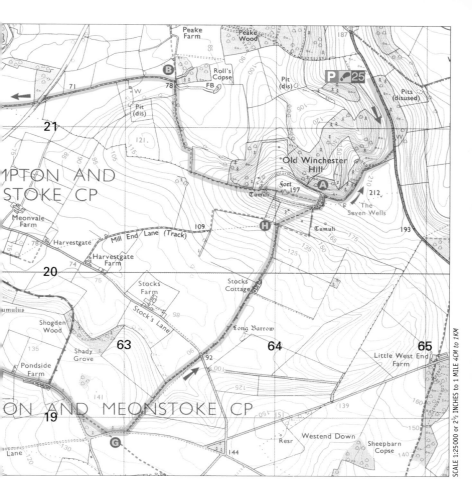

short distance and then turns right over a stile. Cross the field to a stile in the adjoining hedge, then follow this hedge down to a stile that is next to a gate onto a tarmac lane and turn left up the lane **F**.

Follow the lane until you reach a communications tower on the right and take the footpath opposite this into the field on the left. The footpath crosses the corner of the field to leave by a stile onto a tarmac lane on the adjoining hedge. Turn left up the lane **G**.

Take the next footpath, signposted to the left, which leads down the side of a field with the fence on the right. From now on, Old Winchester Hill stands as an indication of the route ahead. Follow the track through a space in the hedge downhill and, on meeting a tarmac road, go straight ahead down a no-through road. This lane runs ahead past a line of cottages, then farm buildings on the right and through a metal field gate. It has now become a wide grass track. Follow this uphill along the right-hand side of the field. On reaching a gate at the top of the field, climb over the stile and take the track that goes diagonally to the right **H**. Go over a stile or through a gate at the top by the fort and take the track around the right-hand side of the fort with a fence on the right. On reaching the track followed at the beginning of the walk **A**, bear right through the gate on the right and follow the cart-track. Then take the grass track on the left, back into the car-parking area.

●

WALK

26

Highland Water, New Forest

Start	Balmer Lawn, Brockenhurst
Distance	8 miles (12.9km)
Approximate time	4½–5 hours
Parking	Forestry Commission Balmer Lawn car park
Refreshments	Pub at Bank on the route or pubs, hotels and cafés at Brockenhurst
Ordnance Survey maps	Landrangers 195 (Bournemouth & Purbeck) and 196 (Solent & the Isle of Wight) and Outdoor Leisure 22 (New Forest)

This walk takes you through scenery typical of the southern section of the New Forest. It is a beautiful woodland walk alongside one of the New Forest's meandering waters that widens to become the Lymington River. The route, starting on the outskirts of Brockenhurst, follows the river through ancient woodland, only leaving it over a footbridge to turn towards the small village of Bank. It departs the village to follow gravel tracks through wood and heath back to the river. The last part of the walk follows the river outside the wood and on heathland. It is advisable to keep dogs on a lead, particularly in May and June.

The route of this walk provides a wonderful chance of seeing deer if you remain quiet and keep dogs on the lead. Even the most gentle dog can become a hunter when the sight or smell of deer brings out the instinct for the chase – specially in summer when fawns are hidden in the bracken by feeding mothers. The result can be fatal.

The New Forest is home to four, or maybe five, types of deer. On this walk you are most likely to see the slim and long-legged summer spotted fallow which are recognisable by a white rump edged with black and a long tail with a black stripe down it. There are also red deer. These are larger, heavier-looking and have a shorter tail and a yellowish-beige rump. If you see a small deer on its own with a white-ruffed, heart-shaped

rump, you are probably looking at a roe.

Leave the car park to cross the road to Beaulieu and walk on the lawn in front of Balmer Lawn Hotel, parallel with the A337 Lyndhurst road, away from Brockenhurst. In the 1939–45 war large forces of troops were marshalled at the Balmer Lawn Hotel as it was the headquarters for the invasion of Europe. Here troops marked the point by erecting an inn sign showing a duck guiding her brood of ducklings into the water.

On reaching a double wicket-gate onto the main road, go through this, cross the road and climb over the stile on the opposite side **A**. Turn right and, when the grass ride divides, take the left-hand ride. As you reach dense woodland, ignore the path on your right and continue ahead with this small

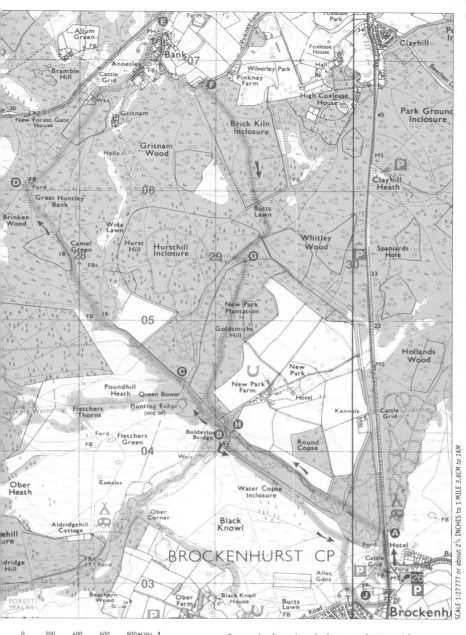

SCALE 1:27777 or about 2¼ INCHES to 1 MILE 3.6CM to 1KM

0	200	400	600	800 METRES	1	
						KILOMETRES MILES
0	200	400	600 YARDS	½		

tightly packed wood on the right. The gravel path then runs alongside fields to the right and the river to the left. New Park, beyond the fields and hidden from view, was a hunting-lodge and is now a hotel. This was one of Charles II's favourite hunting-lodges, and it is said that he brought Nell Gwyn here on several occasions.

Continue to follow this path alongside the river until reaching a wide gravel track. Turn right here **B**. The gravel track soon bears right through a five-bar gate. Ignore this turn and instead go ahead alongside a forest barrier into Queen Bower. This is thought to be the site of a medieval hunting-lodge, named after Eleanor, wife of Edward I. There is no sign of any building but the oak and beech trees here are of an impressive size, some as old as 300 years. The path continues ahead with a fence on the right and the river to the left. When the path splits and there is a footbridge to the left, bear left over the footbridge Ⓒ.

The grassy path now runs alongside the river. You may catch a glimpse of a kingfisher as this river is a popular haunt. The path soon meets a gravel track. If you want a chance to see deer, turn right onto the track, briefly, to a gate that overlooks a fenced-in conservation area. This grazing spot is commonly used by both red and fallow deer. Retrace your steps to continue following the path alongside the river. On the right is a tower hide used for studying the deer.

The path bears right over a bridge. After crossing the footbridge, take the right-hand track, following another section of the river on your right. Follow the riverside for some way until reaching a long, narrow footbridge over it. Turn right to cross the river here Ⓓ.

The grassy path goes straight ahead and uphill. At a fork, take the left-hand grass ride and continue ahead, ignoring paths coming in from the right. Pass a sewage treatment works surrounded by a fence on your left. When a gravel track bends to the left, bear right along a grass path. At a huge fallen tree, bear left and follow a narrow path beside an old tree-stump towards a telegraph pole. Bear left at the pole towards a tarmac road and houses. On reaching the road, bear left to follow it to The Oak pub.

Turn right immediately after the pub Ⓔ to take the road down the side of it. Follow this lane past cottages. It bears to the right, then bends to the left, where there is a cattle-grid. Almost immediately afterwards, a gravel track goes off to the right. Turn onto this, through a side gate Ⓕ.

Ignore grass rides off the track and continue ahead until reaching a T-junction with another gravel track. Bear left here through a gate Ⓖ. Ignore a further gravel track to the left and continue along the main gravel track.

Somewhere in this area was the forest-hut home of Brusher Mills, a well-known local character who lived from 1840 to 1905. He made his name catching snakes, and it is estimated that he caught around 35,000, selling some to a local collector, others to London Zoo and displaying numbers to visitors to the forest. His grave in the church-yard of St Nicholas, Brockenhurst, is visited on Walk 16.

Pass through a side gate next to a five-bar gate and then turn right at a T-junction in the gravel track. Another gate is in sight; go through this and turn left Ⓗ.

This is the track followed prior to entering Queen Bower. Cross the bridge and, just before the end of the wood on the left, turn left to follow an avenue of trees that runs close to the wood edge. The river is on your left. On reaching a narrow gravel track, turn right to go out of the wood and on to the heath. Turn left to follow the grass path along the wood edge. When a narrower path out of the wood crosses this, bear right onto it to cross a footbridge over a narrow stream, then bear left and soon cross a footbridge over the river in front of the Cloud Hotel.

Turn left onto the tarmac road in front of the hotel and follow it back to the main road Ⓙ. Turn left onto the main road for a short distance to cross the road bridge over the river and turn right, back into the car park. ●

Wayfarers' Walk, Ashmansworth

Start	St James's Church, Ashmansworth
Distance	9½ miles (15.3km)
Approximate time	6–6½ hours
Parking	Ashmansworth village
Refreshments	Public houses in Ashmansworth and Hollington Cross
Ordnance Survey maps	Landrangers 174 (Newbury & Wantage) and 185 (Winchester & Basingstoke), Explorer 144 (Basingstoke, Alton & Whitchurch)

This walk, in the far north of Hampshire, starts along a high ridge, part of the Wayfarers' Walk, with wonderful views over both Hampshire and Berkshire. The way begins in the small village of Ashmansworth, then follows an old ox drove to continue along footpaths through fields and along easy-to-walk farm tracks. Part of the route, where the footpaths have become impassable, takes a quiet country lane.

Ashmansworth, the starting point and finishing place on this walk, is the highest village in Hampshire, standing on a ridge at about 770ft (233m) above sea-level. It is a straggling village with houses of typical Hampshire flint and brick, and some thatched cottages. The tiny 12th-century church is well worth a visit. The medieval wall paintings, although only recognisable in small sections, are specially interesting. Erected in the 13th century, the roof of the nave has massive tie-beams which have fascinating carved bosses on the underside. These are said to have come originally from Winchester Cathedral. A modern window has been added in the porch 'In praise of music'. It celebrates English composers and was engraved by Lawrence Whistler in memory of composer Gerald Finzi, who lived in the village.

Leave the church down the track that

Ashmansworth village from the war memorial – the highest village in Hampshire

leads back to the lane and turn left onto this narrow lane. Pass the war memorial and a road to the left. Ignore a road signposted to the right, then one to the left, and continue ahead following the Newbury road. On reaching footpath signs to either side of the road, turn right down the ox drove 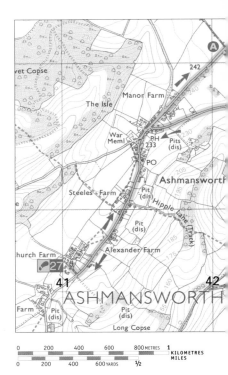Ⓐ.

This track, part of the long-distance Wayfarers' Walk, runs down the side of a field, here with good views to the left. Highclere Castle, the largest mansion in Hampshire, can be clearly seen. The present house, remodelled from a previous one, was built between 1839 and 1842 and designed for the 3rd Earl of Carnarvon by Charles Barry, who was also the architect of the Houses of Parliament. The grounds had been laid out prior to this, in the 1770s, by 'Capability' Brown. The 5th Earl of Carnarvon was a keen egyptologist, and it was he, together with Howard Carter, who discovered Tutankhamun's tomb in 1922. It took six years to empty the tomb of its treasures, including gold masks. By this time the 5th Earl had died of an infected mosquito bite, and his body was brought back to be buried on Beacon Hill, which can be seen from the route. The castle also contains objects from other sites in Egypt.

Highclere Castle is open to the public from Wednesday to Sunday in the afternoons between July and September.

Continue to follow the orange route signs along the North Hampshire Ridgeway, as this path with its superb views is called. When you reach a busy tarmac road cross it carefully, then bear slightly left to cross a secondary road and walk up a well-made cart-track beside a keeper's cottage Ⓑ.

You soon pass a gatehouse on the left. Continue uphill following orange arrows. After going through a metal field gate, cross the field ahead on the

diagonal to go through a gate on the far side onto a farm track. If you look to the left and back you can see Highclere Stud. This was started by the 6th Earl of Carnarvon in 1902. His son, the 7th Earl, continued in the tradition and became racing-manager to the Queen in 1969. Beacon Hill, mentioned earlier, is to the right of the stud. Pheasants are a common sight here for 7000 birds are reared each year on the Highclere estate, where shooting is extremely popular. Continue for a short distance further and then leave the Wayfarers' Walk to turn right uphill following a farm track Ⓒ.

This track leads between hedges to a country lane. On reaching the lane, turn right onto it Ⓓ. Unfortunately, the footpath up the track to the right is too overgrown to follow. The lane goes uphill, then bears to the right. Ignore two lanes off to the left and follow the road ahead, signposted Newbury. Half-way along a straight length of road

there are footpath signs to right and left. The path to the right is the continuation of the overgrown path mentioned earlier. Take the one to the left **E** which crosses the field on a grass path and then winds through some conifers into the next field.

Follow the path along the right-hand side of this field and, on reaching the end of the field, join the cart-track that comes in from the left and then goes straight ahead. Pass the kennels, then cross a tarmac road and take the footpath which is signposted to the right on the other side **F**.

This field path skirts a farm to join the road again by Field House. Pass the house and take the track immediately after it to the left. Cross the road ahead to follow the lane opposite back into the village, turning left at the end to retrace your steps to the start. ●

North New Forest: Fritham to Abbot's Well

Start	Fritham (NB. The A31 Fritham turn-off can be used only when travelling west to east)
Distance	10½ miles (17km). Shorter route 5½ miles (8.9km)
Approximate time	6 hours (3¼ for the shorter route)
Parking	Fritham's Forestry Commission car park, just beyond the Royal Oak pub
Refreshments	Pubs in Frogham or Fritham
Ordnance Survey maps	Landranger 195 (Bournemouth & Purbeck) and Outdoor Leisure 22 (New Forest)

This is a long but easily followed walk which goes almost from the eastern to the western side of the New Forest. As it runs all the way on gravel tracks it is a good route to follow after heavy rain. This northern part of the New Forest mixes both conifer and ancient woodland with heathland, and this path goes through various habitats. Two areas of high heathland provide good views across the neighbouring forest landscape.

In Roman times the woodland inclosures this walk takes you through – Island Thorns, Amberwood and Sloden – were the site of a thriving pottery industry. Clay kilns fired the pottery, and everything required was on hand: clay, sand, water and fuel. Horse and cart transported the fired pots, and the potters lived in wattle huts. In the 5th century, when the Romans left Britain, these potteries were abandoned.

Go back towards the entrance of the car park. Before reaching the entrance there is a gravel track on the left. Take this. Fairly quickly bear right beside a forest barrier and go down a gravel track **Ⓐ**.

Keep to the gravel track which runs downhill. To the right across grass lawn can be seen Eyeworth Pond. This is not a natural pond but was made by damming the water from Irons Well, a spring nearby and another name for the pond. A supply of water was necessary for a neighbouring gunpowder factory, placed here because the ingredients – sulphur, saltpetre and charcoal – could also all be found locally. The factory was started in 1865 and later went on to supply smokeless powder for sportsmen and then gunpowder for use in the 1914–18 war. During its most successful period it employed around a hundred people in seventy mainly wooden buildings. Many of the workers walked long distances across the forest to work in a dangerous business that paid a little extra. Now the pond is popular with picnickers and a wide range of ducks.

As you continue down the track a large red-brick house, surrounded by fields, can also be seen on the right.

Abbot's Well, famous for its pure water, has an uncovered opening for use by forest animals and a covered one for human consumption

This is Eyeworth Lodge, originally a hunting-lodge and later the home of the chemist who ran the gunpowder factory. In the lodge there is a photograph of the local hunt taken a few years ago. To the photographer's surprise when it was developed a ghostly image of an old women in old-fashioned clothing could be seen in the background. Hunting has played a large part in the New Forest's history. At present there are three hunts in the New Forest: the buckhounds, which hunt fallow deer, the foxhounds and the beagles, which go after hares, and each of the three meets twice a week during the winter. The subject provides a basis for strong arguments between local people.

Just before you enter the wood a grassy mound can be seen on the right, obviously containing the remains of a building. This could be an old store for the explosives.

The track bears left and then snakes through the trees and uphill. It then bears right to cross a stream which has been the site for interesting fossil finds. Follow the gravel track as it bears left, ignoring the ride to the right, and continue uphill. When the track divides and goes through a five-bar gate on the left, ignore this route and continue ahead and uphill. A group of holly trees tops the hill on the right. Throughout the forest are names that include the word 'hat'. This is the local name for such a cluster of hollies. The path comes out of the wood. On the left is a gate with side gate. Here a forest keeper's cottage once stood.

The New Forest is divided into twelve beats, each watched over by a keeper who lives on his beat. No one has more intimate knowledge of the wildlife on his patch than the keeper who patrols his area and is responsible for controlling deer numbers. Most are keen conservationists. This keeper's cottage

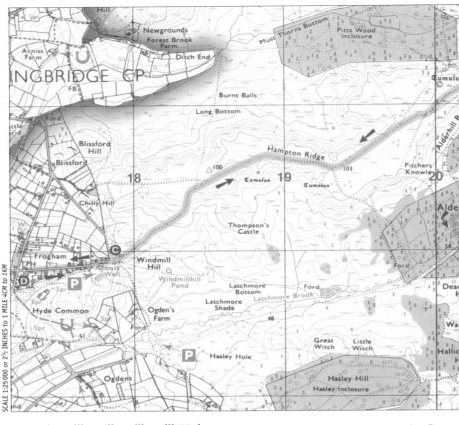

SCALE 1:25000 or 2½ INCHES to 1 MILE 4CM to 1KM

| 0 | 200 | 400 | 600 | 800 METRES | 1 KILOMETRES MILES |
| 0 | 200 | 400 | 600 YARDS | ½ | |

became unused in the 1939–45 war when the area surrounding it became a bombing range and the cottage was destroyed. An old observation post can also be seen on the right. Now it provides valuable shelter to the ponies in bad winter weather.

The path forks at the top of the hill, just by the gates mentioned earlier. Take the left-hand fork which follows the fence line. When a path bears left to continue following the fence **B**, go straight ahead on the gravel track across open ground towards a small mound.

Alternatively, if you want to take the shorter route go along the left-hand path and you soon enter the inclosure to the left by a gate and gravel track. Then continue by following the route after **E** *.*

Continue on the gravel track which follows a route along the top of Hampton Ridge. When the gravel track divides, take the left-hand fork to the left of the mound. There are fine views to right and left. In all but the driest weather a pond can be seen below on the left, with Latchmoor Brook beyond. This is Windmillhill Pond which features in *Wanderers in the New Forest*, the story of the period that Juliette de Bairacli-Levy, a traveller and herbalist, spent with her children living in a New Forest cabin close to Abbot's Well. It was here, or in the brook, that the family bathed almost every day in winter as well as in summer.

Continue along the track towards a group of houses. On reaching the tarmac road which goes to the right and straight ahead, join the road straight ahead **C**.

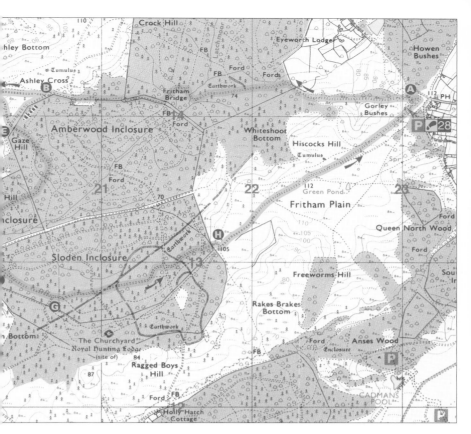

On the corner is Abbot's Well with two drinking holes, one for the animals and one covered for human use. The water from this well is reputed to be the finest in the New Forest, and the gypsies consider it to have health-giving properties. Follow the road uphill to the Forester's Arms which is well known locally for good food and real ale **D**.

Leave the pub and retrace your footsteps along Hampton Ridge as far as the mound. Just after passing this and reaching a group of small oaks on the left, turn right down a gravel track. This goes through the heather to a gate into the conifer inclosure **E**.

Enter the inclosure by the wicket-gate and go downhill. Ignore the first gravel track on the left and continue downhill between oaks and conifers. When the main track swings to the left and another one continues ahead, follow the main track left. The path goes over a bridge then out of the inclosure. Cross a wide grass track, past a pony pound, explained under Walk 3, and through the gate into the inclosure on the other side.

When the track divides and a path goes off to the left, continue straight ahead **F**.

The track divides again. Here one section goes off to the right and out of the inclosure through a gate. Instead, continue through the wood on the path that bears slightly to the left **G**.

This gravel track snakes uphill through the trees to leave the inclosure finally through a gate. Almost immediately the gravel track splits again. Bear left **H**.

The route now takes you across Fritham Plain. After about 1 mile (1.6km) the track reaches bushes and a forest barrier. The path then divides. Continue ahead back into the car park. ●

Further Information

Long-distance Paths

Hampshire County Council, who are responsible for all rights of way in the county, have established a system of special long-distance paths. These are distinctively signposted, waymarked and maintained to ensure that they are easy to follow. There are eight paths in all, criss-crossing the county, and they have been designed both to connect places of interest and to pass through beautiful countryside.

1 The Solent Way, 60 miles (96km), runs along the coast from Christchurch to Emsworth.
2 The Wayfarers' Walk, 70 miles (113km), goes diagonally north–south from Inkpen Beacon to near Portsmouth.
3 The South Downs Way, a national trail, is 90 miles (145km) long and runs east from Winchester to Eastbourne.
4 The Hangers Way, 17 miles (27km), follows the Hampshire Hangers, steep-sided hills that run north from Petersfield to Alton.
5 The Test Way, 46 miles (74km) long, runs mainly along the Test valley from Totton to Inkpen Beacon.
6 The Clarendon Way, which is 24 miles (39km) in length, goes from Salisbury to Winchester.
7 The Staunton Way, 14 miles (22.5km), runs from Queen Elizabeth Country Park to Havant.
8 The Avon Valley Path is 34 miles (55km) long and follows the Avon valley from Salisbury to Christchurch.

Sections of many of these paths form part of routes in this book but, having done these walks, why not follow some of the long-distance routes either walking one complete route over a few days or doing just a short section at a time.

Hampshire County Councils' Country-side and Community Department have free leaflets on all the paths, except the Wayfarers' Walk on which there is a booklet. The leaflets are available from local tourist information centres and some libraries, or send a stamped addressed envelope to the address on page 95.

Hampshire Wildlife Trust

Hampshire is a county specially rich in wildlife. It probably has more species of wild flowering plants than any other county in Britain and even has some rare plants and animals that can only be found in Hampshire. Two of these are wild gladioli and New Forest cicadas. We still have small numbers of some now very rare species. Otters are still found in two sites. Although you are unlikely to see very rare plants or animals on these walks, if you keep your eyes open and your ears well tuned, each walk should provide you with something of particular interest to enrich the experience.

Hampshire Wildlife Trust, responsible for so much conservation in the area, owns or manages fifty nature reserves, which cover 4000 acres (1600ha) of countryside. Of these nature reserves 91 per cent is considered so vital for wildlife that the areas are recognised as Sites of Special Scientific Interest. The majority of these reserves are open to the public, at least in part. Some require permits, and visitors are asked to respect wildlife and keep to paths in all of them.

If you would like to become more closely involved in protecting Hampshire's wildlife, or require more information on the reserves, contact Hampshire Wildlife Trust at the address on page 95.

The National Trust

Anyone who likes visiting places of natural beauty and/or historic interest has cause to be grateful to the National Trust. Without it, many such places would probably have vanished by now.

It was in response to the pressures on the countryside posed by the relentless march of Victorian industrialisation that the trust was set up in 1895. Its founders, inspired by the common goals of protecting and conserving Britain's national heritage and widening public access to it, were Sir Robert Hunter, Octavia Hill and Canon Rawnsley: respectively a solicitor, a social reformer and a clergyman. The latter was particularly influential. As a canon of Carlisle Cathedral and vicar of Crosthwaite (near Keswick), he was concerned about threats to the Lake District and had already been active in protecting footpaths and promoting public access to open countryside. After the flooding of Thirlmere in 1879 to create a large reservoir, he became increasingly convinced that the only effective way to guarantee protection was outright ownership of land.

The purpose of the National Trust is to preserve areas of natural beauty and sites of historic interest by acquisition, holding them in trust for the nation and making them available for public access and enjoyment. Some of its properties have been acquired through purchase, but many have been donated. Nowadays it is not only one of the biggest landowners in the country, but also one of the most active conservation charities, protecting 581,113 acres (253,176 ha) of land, including 555 miles (892km) of coastline, and over 300 historic properties in England, Wales and Northern Ireland. (There is a separate National Trust for Scotland, which was set up in 1931.)

Furthermore, once a piece of land has come under National Trust ownership, it is difficult for its status to be altered. As a result of parliamentary legislation in 1907, the Trust was given the right to declare its property inalienable, so ensuring that in any subsequent dispute it can appeal directly to parliament.

As it works towards its dual aims of conserving areas of attractive countryside and encouraging greater public access (not easy to reconcile in this age of mass

Clearings in Micheldever Wood provide space for wild flowers, which in turn entice butterflies

tourism), the Trust provides an excellent service for walkers by creating new concessionary paths and waymarked trails, maintaining stiles and footbridges and combating the ever-increasing problem of footpath erosion.

For details of membership, contact the National Trust at the address on page 95.

 ## The Ramblers' Association

No organisation works more actively to protect and extend the rights and interests of walkers in the countryside than the Ramblers' Association. Its aims are clear: to foster a greater knowledge, love and care of the countryside; to assist in the protection and enhancement of public rights of way and areas of natural beauty; to work for greater public access to the countryside; and to encourage more people to take up rambling as a healthy, recreational leisure activity.

It was founded in 1935 when, following the setting up of a National Council of Ramblers' Federations in 1931, a number of federations earlier formed in London, Manchester, the Midlands and elsewhere came together to create a more effective pressure group, to deal with such problems as the disappearance and obstruction of footpaths, the prevention of access to open mountain and moorland and increasing hostility from landowners. This was the era of the mass trespasses, when there were sometimes violent confrontations between ramblers and gamekeepers, especially on the moorlands of the Peak District.

Since then the Ramblers' Association has played an influential role in preserving and developing the national footpath network, supporting the creation of national parks and encouraging the designation and waymarking of long-distance routes.

Our freedom to walk in the countryside is precarious and requires constant vigilance. As well as the perennial problems of footpaths being illegally obstructed, disappearing through lack of use or extinguished by housing or road construction, new dangers can spring up at any time.

It is to meet such problems and dangers that the Ramblers' Association exists and represents the interests of all walkers. The address to write to for information on the Ramblers' Association and how to become a member is given on page 95.

Walkers and the Law

The average walker in a national park or other popular walking area, armed with the appropriate Ordnance Survey map, reinforced perhaps by a guidebook giving detailed walking instructions, is unlikely to run into legal difficulties, but it is useful to know something about the law relating to public rights of way. The right

to walk over certain parts of the countryside has developed over a long period, and how such rights came into being is a complex subject, too lengthy to be discussed here. The following comments are intended simply as a helpful guide, backed up by the Countryside Access Charter, a concise summary of walkers' rights and obligations drawn up by the Countryside Agency.

Basically there are two main kinds of public rights of way: footpaths (for walkers only) and bridleways (for walkers, riders on horseback and pedal cyclists). Footpaths and bridleways are shown by broken green lines on Ordnance Survey Pathfinder and Outdoor Leisure maps and broken red lines on Landranger maps. There is also a third category, called byways: chiefly broad tracks (green lanes) or farm roads, which walkers, riders and cyclists have to share, usually only occasionally, with motor vehicles. Many of these public paths have been in existence for hundreds of years and some even originated as prehistoric trackways and have been in constant use for well over 2000 years. Ways known as RUPPs (roads used as public paths) still appear on some maps. The legal definition of such byways is ambiguous and they are gradually being reclassified as footpaths, bridleways or byways.

The term 'right of way' means exactly what it says. It gives right of passage over what, in the vast majority of cases, is private land, and you are required to keep to the line of the path and not stray on to the land on either side. If you inadvertently wander off the right of way – either because of faulty map-reading or because the route is not clearly indicated on the ground – you are technically trespassing and the wisest course is to ask the nearest available person (farmer or fellow walker) to direct you back to the correct route. There are stories about unpleasant

A footbridge on the Bishop's Dyke walk

Countryside Access Charter

Your rights of way are:

- public footpaths – on foot only. Sometimes waymarked in yellow
- bridleways – on foot, horseback and pedal cycle. Sometimes waymarked in blue
- byways (usually old roads), most 'roads used as public paths' and, of course, public roads – all traffic has the right of way

Use maps, signs and waymarks to check rights of way. Ordnance Survey Pathfinder and Landranger maps show most public rights of way

On rights of way you can:

- take a pram, pushchair or wheelchair if practicable
- take a dog (on a lead or under close control)
- take a short route round an illegal obstruction or remove it sufficiently to get past

You have a right to go for recreation to:

- public parks and open spaces – on foot
- most commons near older towns and cities – on foot and sometimes on horseback
- private land where the owner has a formal agreement with the local authority

In addition you can use the following by local or established custom or consent, but ask for advice if you are unsure:

- many areas of open country, such as moorland, fell and coastal areas, especially those in the care of the National Trust, and some commons
- some woods and forests, especially those owned by the Forestry Commission
- country parks and picnic sites
- most beaches
- canal towpaths
- some private paths and tracks Consent sometimes extends to horse-riding and cycling

For your information:

- county councils and London boroughs maintain and record rights of way, and register commons
- obstructions, dangerous animals, harassment and misleading signs on rights of way are illegal and you should report them to the county council
- paths across fields can be ploughed, but must normally be reinstated within two weeks
- landowners can require you to leave land to which you have no right of access
- motor vehicles are normally permitted only on roads, byways and some 'roads used as public paths'

---

confrontations between walkers and farmers at times, but in general most farmers are co-operative when responding to a genuine and polite request for assistance in route-finding.

Obstructions can sometimes be a problem and probably the most common of these is where a path across a field has been ploughed up. It is legal for a farmer to plough up a path provided that he restores it within two weeks, barring exceptionally bad weather. This does not always happen and here the walker is presented with a dilemma: to follow the line of the path, even if this inevitably means treading on crops, or to walk around the edge of the field. The latter

course of action often seems the best but this means that you would be trespassing and not keeping to the exact line of the path. In the case of other obstructions which may block a path (illegal fences and locked gates etc), common sense has to be used in order to negotiate them by the easiest method – detour or removal. You should only ever remove as much as is necessary to get through, and if you can easily go round the obstruction without causing any damage, then you should do so. If you have any problems negotiating rights of way, you should report the matter to the rights of way department of the relevant council, which will take action with the landowner concerned.

Apart from rights of way enshrined by law, there are a number of other paths available to walkers. Permissive or concessionary paths have been created where a landowner has given permission for the public to use a particular route across his land. The main problem with these is that, as they have been granted as a concession, there is no legal right to use them and therefore they can be extinguished at any time. In practice, many of these concessionary routes have been established on land owned either by large public bodies such as the Forestry Commission, or by a private one, such as the National Trust, and as these mainly encourage walkers to use their paths, they are unlikely to be closed unless a change of ownership occurs.

Walkers also have free access to country parks (except where requested to keep away from certain areas for ecological reasons, eg. wildlife protection, woodland regeneration, safeguarding of rare plants etc), canal towpaths and most beaches. By custom, though not by right, you are generally free to walk across the open and uncultivated higher land of mountain, moorland and fell, but this varies from area to area and from one season to another – grouse moors, for example, will be out of bounds during the breeding and shooting seasons and some open areas are used as Ministry of Defence firing ranges, for which reason access will be restricted. In some areas the situation has been clarified as a result of 'access agreements' between the landowners and either the county council or the national park authority, which clearly define when and where you can walk over such open country.

 Walking Safety

Although the reasonably gentle countryside that is the subject of this book offers no real dangers to walkers at any time of the year, it is still advisable to take sensible precautions and follow certain well-tried guidelines.

Always take with you both warm and waterproof clothing and sufficient food and drink. Wear suitable footwear, i.e. strong walking boots or shoes that give a good grip over stony ground, on slippery slopes and in muddy conditions. Try to obtain a local weather forecast and bear it in mind before you start. Do not be afraid to abandon your proposed route and return to your starting point in the event of a sudden and unexpected deterioration in the weather.

All the walks described in this book will be safe to do, given due care and respect, even during the winter. Indeed, a crisp, fine winter day often provides perfect walking conditions, with firm ground underfoot and a clarity unique to this time of the year.

The most difficult hazard likely to be encountered is mud, especially when walking along woodland and field paths, farm tracks and bridleways – the latter in particular can often get churned up by cyclists and horses. In summer, an additional difficulty may be narrow and overgrown paths, particularly along the edges of cultivated fields. Neither should constitute a major problem provided that the appropriate footwear is worn.

 Useful Organisations

Council for the Protection of Rural England
25 Buckingham Palace Road, London SW1W 0PP. Tel. 020 7976 6433

Countryside Agency
John Dower House, Crescent Place, Cheltenham, Gloucestershire GL50 3RA. Tel. 01242 521381

Forestry Commission
Information Branch, 231 Corstorphine Road, Edinburgh EH12 7AT. Tel. 0131 334 0303
Forest Enterprise, South Downs District, Bucks Horn Oak, Farnham, Surrey GU10 4LS. Tel. 01420 23666; Fax: 01420 22082

Hampshire County Council
Rights-of-Way Section
Countryside and Community Department,
Mottisfont Court, High Street,
Winchester, Hampshire SO23 8ZF.
Tel. 01962 846002

Hampshire Wildlife Trust
8 Romsey Road, Eastleigh,
Hampshire SO50 9AL.
Tel. 023 8061 3636/3737

Long Distance Walkers' Association
21 Upcroft, Windsor,
Berkshire SL4 3NH.
Tel. 01753 866685

National Trust
Membership and general enquiries:
PO Box 39, Bromley, Kent BR1 3XL.
Tel. 020 8315 9111
Southern Regional Office:
Polesden Lacey, Dorking, Surrey RH5 6BD.
Tel. 01372 453401

Ordnance Survey
Romsey Road, Maybush,
Southampton SO16 4GU.
Tel. 08456 05 05 05 (Lo-call)

Ramblers' Association
1–5 Wandsworth Road, London SW8 2XX.
Tel. 020 7339 8500

Southern Tourist Board
40 Chamberlayne Road,
Eastleigh SO5 5JH.
Tel. 023 8062 0006

Local tourist information numbers:
(*not open all year):
Aldershot: 01252 320968
Alton: 01420 88448
Andover: 01264 324320
Basingstoke: 01256 817618
Eastleigh: 023 8064 1261
Fareham: 01329 221342/824896
Fleet: 01252 811151
*Fordingbridge: 01425 654560
Gosport: 023 9252 2944
Havant: 023 9248 0024
*Hayling Island: 023 9246 7111
*Lymington: 01590 672422
Lyndhurst and New Forest: 023 8028 2269
Petersfield: 01730 268829
Portsmouth, The Hard: 023 9282 6722
*Ringwood: 01425 470896

Romsey: 01794 512987
Rownhams (M27): 023 8073 0345
Southampton: 023 8022 1106
Winchester: 01962 840500/848180

Youth Hostels Association
Trevelyan House, 8 St Stephen's Hill,
St Albans, Hertfordshire AL1 2DY.
Tel. 01727 855215

 ### Ordnance Survey Maps of Hampshire and the New Forest

Hampshire is covered by Ordnance Survey 1:50 000 scale (2cm to 1km or $1\frac{1}{4}$ inches to 1 mile) Landranger sheets 184, 185, 186, 195, 196 and 197. These all-purpose maps are packed with information to help you explore the area. Viewpoints, picnic sites, places of interest, caravan and camping sites are shown, as well as public rights of way information such as footpaths and bridleways.

To examine Hampshire in more detail, and especially if you are planing walks, Ordnance Survey Explorer maps at 1:25 000 scale (4cm to 1km or $2\frac{1}{2}$ inches to 1 mile) are ideal. Maps covering this area are:

119 (Meon Valley, Portsmouth, Gosport & Fareham)
112 (Chichester, South Harting & Selsey)
130 (Salisbury & Stonehenge)
131 (Romsey, Andover & Test Valley)
132 (Winchester, New Alresford & East Meon)
133 (Haslemere & Petersfield)
144 (Basingstoke, Alton & Whitchurch)
158 (Newbury & Hungerford)
159 (Reading, Wokingham & Pangbourne)

Outdoor Leisure map 22 (New Forest) covers part of Hampshire and is also at 1:25 000 scale ($2\frac{1}{2}$ inches to 1 mile) scale.

To get to Hampshire, use the Ordnance Survey Travelmaster map number 9 South East England at 1:250 000 scale (1cm to 2.5km or 1 inch to 4 miles).

Ordnance Survey maps and guides are available from most booksellers, stationers and newsagents.

Index

Entries in italics refer to illustrations